Staging Luxurious Homes

Finding, Attracting and Serving Affluent Prospects and Clients

By Barbara Jennings, CSS/CRS

D1065603

Copyright

Barbara Jennings, CSS/CRS
Author/Consultant/Trainer

LIBRARY OF CONGRESS NUMBER: TX6-501-524
ISBN 978-0-9618026-3-9   PRINTED IN THE USA

Disclaimer

This manual is designed to provide accurate information with respect to the subject matter covered. It is sold with the understanding that the publisher and author are not engaged in rendering legal, insurance, marketing or other professional services, nor do they guarantee any level of profits any individual reader/trainee might derive. If legal advice or other expert assistance is needed, the services of a competent attorney or professional person specializing in that field should be sought. Purchasers and users of the information contained in this manual do so at their own risk and neither author nor publishers shall be held liable for any circumstance arising out of the use of this material or for conducting business of any sort as a result of information contained in this manual. While every attempt has been made to provide accurate information, the author and publisher cannot be held responsible for errors or omissions. Some of the information regarding actual clients has been altered because of privacy issues, therefore all names and facts are to be regarded as fictitious. Any resemblance to actual persons or businesses is purely coincidental.

Table of Contents

Dedication

Leone Cole

Many of you know that during the writing of this book, my 94 year old mother broke her hip. She lives in Japan and spent 3 months in a Japanese hospital, enduring cold food for every meal, numerous complications including blood clots, loneliness, depression and great pain.

But she pulled through and is currently back in her home in Tokyo, though we don't know if she will ever walk again. With the help of my brother and his wife and some government sponsored programs to the elderly, she is coping with life in a wheel chair.

So it seemed appropriate to dedicate this book to one of the most influential persons in my life. Always a hard worker and a woman of great dedication, patience, perseverance and courage, she has been a fabulous role model for me, serving as a Christian missionary for over 60 years, even after my Dad died nearly 30 years ago.

Though she would not classify as a member of the affluent society, and though she lives in a very old, very modest home built by other missionaries, she is rich in spirit and loved by many.

To you, Mom.

Chapter 1
Who Are the Affluent?

Introduction

Before we can really understand how to approach the affluent
marketplace, we need to define what that means. In this book, I will be
using the words affluent, upscale, luxury and wealthy interchangeably.
That's in part to vary the text and in part to speak to you in multiple
ways as I tackle this complex and intriguing group of consumers. I also
recognize that these words mean different things to different people and
much of that will depend on your own personal social standing and how
you see yourself in comparison to the rest of the world. For some,
affluent is equivalent with being "rich". To others, affluent is equivalent
to being "extremely rich" or "insanely rich". To others it merely means
having wealth that is above and beyond the norm. And since the norm

keeps changing, so do the definitions of upscale, affluent, luxury, rich and wealthy.

In the eighties, the rich or wealthy were identified by William Davis, in his book The Rich, as:

- **Rich** - $3 million to $14 million
- **Very Rich** - Over $14 million to $50 million
- **Super Rich** - Over $50 million to $100 million
- **Can't Count** (the Getty definition) - any family worth more than $100 million

But that has all changed by this writing, and even by the end of this year, it will have changed again. Bill Gates, the owner and developer of the Windows platform and many other computer systems and programs, is the wealthiest man in the world. He is now reported to be worth in excess of $100 Billion dollars and there are now hundreds of billionaires all over the world, though it is generally accepted that Bill Gates is the richest individual on the planet. And these are just estimates, for it is really impossible to calculate the true worth of the richest people or families on the planet.

Our favorite movie stars and professional athletes are generally considered to be very wealthy as well as famous. Politicians tend to be wealthy. Heads of major corporations are wealthy. But many would consider anyone making over $100,000 per year to be wealthy, and indeed, making over $100,000 per year does put one in a category which consists of a small percentage of Americans.

Some are wealthy with money; others are wealthy by way of possessions (land, art, etc); some are wealthy by ownership (stocks, bonds, property).

Definitions

For the purposes of this tutorial, however, when in referring to the wealthy I use the term "upscale", I am not referring to the richest people on the planet. There are too few of them to base a business on, plus they are difficult to contact and, even if you do, more difficult to impress. These types of individuals must find you. Not the other way around.

There are far, far more people who fall into the "upscale" definition who can and should become your clients.

According to the census bureau, the median income in the United States by state was:

1. Connecticut $56,409
2. New Jersey $56,356
3. Maryland $54,302
4. Massachusetts $52,713
5. New Hampshire $52,409
6. Alaska $52,391
7. Minnesota $50,750
8. Virginia $50,028
9. Colorado $49,248
10. Delaware $48,770
11. California $48,440
12. Hawaii $48,274
13. Washington $48,185
14. Illinois $47,367
15. Utah $46,709
16. Wisconsin $46,538
17. Michigan $46,291
18. Nevada $45,249
19. Rhode Island $45,006
20. New York $44,139
21. Indiana $43,323
22. **United States Median $43,318**
23. District of Columbia $43,215
24. Ohio $43,119
25. Kansas $43,113
26. Pennsylvania $42,952
27. Vermont $42,649
28. Oregon $42,593
29. Georgia $42,421
30. Iowa $42,278
31. Nebraska $41,984
32. Arizona $41,963
33. Wyoming $41,554
34. Missouri $40,870
35. Texas $39,967
36. Idaho $39,859
37. North Carolina $39,438
38. Maine $39,212
39. Florida $38,985
40. North Dakota $38,223
41. South Dakota $38,008
42. South Carolina $38,003
43. Tennessee $37,925
44. Kentucky $36,663
45. Alabama $36,131
46. Oklahoma $35,634
47. New Mexico $35,091
48. Montana $34,449
49. Louisiana $33,792
50. Arkansas $33,445
51. West Virginia $32,967
52. Mississippi $32,397

Source: Census Bureau

As you can see, the average for the country is #22 - $43,318. All of these figures need to be adjusted upward since then as the cost of living rises each year. So any person or family whose income is significantly higher than the median (in your part of the country) should be considered an "upscale" client. That is your target market.

For more recent research, consider that:

"The super rich (with annual household incomes of $200,000+:
Includes about 2.5 million households, or about 2% of the population.
About 1/3rd are over 55, so their wealth will not likely come from
monthly salaries. About 80% live in family situations with spouses and
children. The super rich include businesspeople and experienced
professionals. Many come from the entertainment industry.

Of course, people tend not to think of themselves as being the super
rich. So you'll often hear this definition given as pertaining to anyone
whose "invest-able income" exceeds $1,000,000. You see, there's a big
difference between making $1,000,000 in gross income and having
$1,000,000 available to invest. Of course, there is a category above
them – you know – those household names like Bill Gates, Donald Trump
and the like. Now we're talking multi millionaires and billionaires.

**"The affluent (with annual household incomes of $100,000 to
$199,000:** Includes about 10.5 million households, or about 10% of the
population. Most are 45 to 54 and live in large metro areas. However,
about 12.1 percent of affluent households are headed by an individual
under 35. Though Asian Americans constitute only 3 percent of the

population, they represent 5 percent of affluent households. Blacks make up 5.7 percent, and Whites account for 86%. Physicians, financial analysts, and investment bankers are frequently in this category.

"The near affluent (with annual household incomes of $75,000 to $99,000: Includes about 10.8 million households or about 10 percent of the population. This group has done well in recent years, growing from 5 percent in 1990. Most are 35 and up.

But when we factor in the cost of living and inflation, these numbers seem low to me as of this writing. $100,000 will not buy nearly as much today as it did 20 years ago. For that matter, $1,000,000 (the symbol of real success and achievement) is not really a very good measure of extreme wealth any more – for the same reasons.

So when comparing data and totals of consumers in each of these groups, one must always keep in mind that it is much easier to attain the level of millionaire today – but at the same time it doesn't have the same value as it did 40 years ago. To have a similar value to what it meant 40 years ago, one really has to make $10,000,000 today, give or take a few bucks.

In the 1960's when I was a young career woman, gasoline was 33 cents per gallon. Now it's usually over $3.00 per gallon here in California. That's a pretty significant difference. And bear in mind that gasoline has been one of the least inflation responsive products on the market. One only has to look at the skyrocketing increase in medical costs, the price of automobiles and homes to see the effects of inflation.

The Cream of the Crop

I think it would be a fair assumption, over all, to say that the affluent, wealthy consumer is generally well educated, focused, talented, and considered among the cream of the crop. That is to say, this would be fair of those that earned their wealth. It might not be as true of those that inherited their wealth. So dealing with this group of consumers you'll have to be "on top of your game", because these people are sharp, have high expectations (not only of themselves but of others), and they can also be demanding.

Vehicles of the Affluent

Interestingly enough, the affluent often do not drive the kind of vehicles one might expect them to drive. Depending on which part of the country they reside in, they have a large tendency to drive more moderate vehicles, not wanting to flaunt or expose their true financial status. So, generally speaking, you're not going to find most of them driving around town in a Mercedes or Jaguar or other type of status vehicle.

On the other hand, you'll often see people in much lower economic brackets buying the high priced, status vehicles – vehicles that far exceed their ability to support. Part of the reason for that is that the vehicle may be the only way they can look successful. People who are struggling financial usually can't afford to purchase a home of their own, so instead they purchase an expensive car. I point this out because one should therefore not look at the vehicle a person drives as being any kind of accurate measure of their true financial status.

I myself don't pay attention to the types of cars my neighbors drive, nor my clients either. But my husband and male associate and son are very aware of what other people drive. Guess it's a guy thing. I'm more apt to look at wardrobe, quality of home, handbag. But that can be deceiving too.

Types of Small Businesses

Statistics also show that the majority of wealthy, affluent consumers own their own small businesses. One might think they would be corporate executives, but the greatest majority of them are entrepreneurs. So if you had any doubts about starting your own business, you should know that you are on the right path and are already giving yourself the best possible opportunity to attain your financial dreams.

And statistics also show that it doesn't matter what industry you go into. There are plenty of wealthy business owners in every conceivable industry. There is no single industry that has an overabundance of wealthy owners, though there are some industries that might turn out to be more profitable by a small margin.

I believe that one of the keys to achieving great success in your chosen field is to first love what you do. When you love what you do, you will naturally be more enthusiastic and you will probably devote more time and energy to your business. Without a great deal of time and energy invested, the average small business would fail because very few businesses start out "hot".

Some people get lucky and strike it rich immediately. But for the rest of us, building a really profitable business has required time, patience, dedication and perseverance. More on this later.

Listen to the Industry Experts

What's the best way to key into the luxury market and begin acquiring clients who can afford top-of-the-line products, one-of-a-kind designs, and home staging services? It's no secret any more.

If you have not acquired my basic home staging tutorial, **Home Staging for Profit** (http://www.decorate-redecorate.com/home-staging-training.html) or my basic interior redesign tutorial, **Rearrange It** (http://www.decorate-redecorate.com/rearrange.html), then I highly suggest you get one or the other of these ebooks or manuals to augment your training. These tutorials will teach you all the basics and the necessary information to launch and set up your business along with providing you with all of the business forms. You can't afford to miss this training for it will ground you firmly in your staging or redesign business whether you're working with clients in the low or moderate income level or with the affluent.

Implementing a "Preferred Client Business Strategy" can help re-designers and stagers build a client base of more upscale clients. This strategy revolves around targeting the right clients, engaging in effective

business strategies and maximizing referrals from the types of clients most likely to bring highly profitable projects to your business.

The key to success is zeroing in on Baby Boomers (those my age and a little younger), the generation that possesses the largest disposable income in history – largely made up of entrepreneurs who made it because of their excellent work ethics, creativity and ingenuity. Couple this with the fact that aging Boomers have fewer personal obligations since their children have grown up and have left home, and since they also have a high interest in acquiring secondary incomes, and it becomes clear the Baby Boomers constitute a growing and attractive target market for a staging or redesign business.

If you live in or near a resort area, you can expect to see a huge up-swell of older consumers looking to buy, lease, time share or rent secondary homes, even if they only plan to use them a few weeks each year. We'll be reading more and more about this in the coming years, so positioning your staging and redesign services for this market now would be very smart indeed.

Become a specialist to a group within the overall group. For instance, if you live near or in Tahoe, a popular resort area, become the "go-to" person for everything having to do with visiting, buying, selling, or decorating in that community. Become the source of information for that resort area, and you'll be amazed at how people start coming to you and asking you to work with them, rather than the other way around.

Where younger generations can easily postpone decorating or selling a home when an unfavorable economic climate or financial concern arises, 55-year-old empty nesters can't (or won't) - it's their moment and they have to go for it before they have health issues, or other life circumstances which diminish their freedom.

So, even if there is a decrease in the low to middle income bracket, the luxury client will continue to buy and sell and decorate. And in today's remodeling boom, the upper end of the market is growing more quickly than the mainstream. Even in a slow real estate market, the wealthy keep on doing business as usual in most cases.

Another reason for you to focus on older high-end clients is the fact that the lower the budget, the more the client wants control of selecting the products and controlling the pricing of everything. Haggling over the price of your services is more likely to happen with the mainstream client and less likely with the affluent client. Busy upscale consumers are more comfortable with letting a designer or stager manage a project for them. This means less time spent holding their hands, so to speak, and educating a client. The affluent homeowner just wants to get it done. They expect quality and service, but they are very protective of their time and energy, so they are much more willing to turn the reins over to persons they regard as professionals than any other segment of society.

A simple strategy for successfully building a base of upscale clients centers on increasing the size of an average sale, as well as on improving the closing rate by asking effective qualifying questions. Statistics also show that people who entertain frequently are the most likely purchasers of decorating products and services.

Naturally if a client entertains a lot, there is a higher degree of wanting the home to look spectacular and impressive. So one of the best questions you can ask is, "How often do you entertain?" It's not an invasive, personal question like matters dealing with income, and it will certainly give you a clear idea of what their likely interest in decorating and staging will be.

For this reason, upscale salespeople make excellent prospects for your staging and redesign services. These are people who have probably been taught the value of entertaining in their home. They do it to build relationships with their prospects. So you stand an excellent chance of not only getting them as a client, but getting them to refer you to their client base as well.

Breaking It Down

So let's break down the different types of wealthy consumers out there so that you will understand more fully how they got their wealth. Later we will discuss other issues pertinent to how they spend their income. I will also discuss the most likely time they will be in a spending mode.

Generators of Wealth

The consumer who generates wealth is an entrepreneur, just like you. He or she has spent a considerable amount of time and energy building a business of their own. As I said earlier, the small business owner of today is more likely to have spend-able wealth than any other group and that is one major reason the health and prosperity of small business is so vital to the country. Of the small business owners, 10% dominate the market. Therefore you want to concentrate on those that created a growing business that has lasted for 10 years or more and whose owners are 50 years or order.

The owner of a company stands a much better chance of reaching the pinnacle of success in their field because they are usually more vitally interested in the industry and are usually more willing to work long hours to achieve their goals. They are also more likely to take risks and think outside the box. They are a special breed of people. They know what it takes to become successful and they are largely people who attained their wealth without much help from others.

They are also people who naturally respect other entrepreneurs, especially those that are professional and who recognize the importance of offering a quality product or service and backing it with outstanding customer service.

You might consider positioning yourself as the home stager to the small business owner, or the interior re-designer to the small business owner. You could put together information packets and a website that cater just to this type of client. You could attend the kinds of meetings, clubs, social events, community groups and industry conferences and conventions that small business owners attend.

You'll find that most of the top achievers of small business are professionals from:

- Medical profession
- Consultants
- Engineers
- Attorneys
- Architects
- Chefs

- Airline Pilots
- Coaches
- Artists
- Entertainers
- Professional athletes

For many of these successful professionals, their business will have little value when they retire and they know they have to fund their own retirement. Many of them have agents or employees who serve as gatekeepers. This makes it harder to reach them. Some live flamboyant lifestyles. They might even be considered unstable. Some make a huge amount of money from product endorsements and personal appearances. They will usually have agents, attorneys and managers who screen those wanting to contact them.

So for many of these types of wealthy prospects, the road to contact is difficult, but well worth the effort when you succeed.

Earners of Wealth

A smaller group, but still very sizeable, are your top key executives who are employees for corporations and major businesses. Add to that the top producing salespeople who are usually on commissions. Those few executives who reach the top of the corporate ladder are earners of vast sums of money, as are the top salespeople in a wide range of industries.

It's not unheard of for top executives of major corporations to earn millions of dollars each year, with phenomenal bonuses built into their contracts. Super successful salespeople on commission usually have a steady stream of income, but there are always those who have a windfall profit from a really large sale from time to time.

You could target a specific industry that is thriving in your part of the country and contact all of the top performers among that industry. Build a reputation as being the "go to" person for that industry. If you live in a rural area, contact the top farmers and ranchers in the area. If you live in a metropolitan area, become a specialist to the computer industry, the insurance industry, the auto industry, the financial services industry and others.

You could become the top stager or re-designer for the American Bar Association, the United Fresh Fruits and Vegetables Association, the International Fabricare Institute or the Associated General Contractors of America.

Did you know that crane operators are among the mostly highly paid employees, according to the New York Times? But I bet no stager or re-designer has ever targeted them as an industry group. It is reported that there are more affluent blue collar workers in America than there are dentists. Many make over $400,000 per year. Writing articles for their trade publication could become pretty lucrative, don't you think? And how much competition do you think you'd have?

Rather than trying to be all things to all people, specialize in a particular industry. That way you can gain a reputation easier and become highly knowledgeable on issues that are pertinent and of vital interest to your client base. This will also help you guard against new competition moving in to your area. Most people target too broad a market when specialization could be the key to great financial rewards.

Here is a brief list of some specific categories you might consider targeting:

1. Attorneys
2. Plumbers
3. Heating and Air Conditioning Service Providers
4. Beverage Wholesalers
5. Insurance Salespeople
6. Marketing Salespeople
7. Entrepreneurs of all Industries
8. Physicians
9. Healthcare Industry in General
10. Vacation/Time Share Businesses
11. Internet Marketers

Inheritors of Wealth

Then there are those that have great wealth who did not earn it themselves. They inherited the wealth or it was given to them for some reason, or they won the lottery. Widows live an average of 7 years longer than their husbands and many of them haven't been that involved in the process of how the money was made, but they are now in charge of it. They often want to consolidate and simplify their lives, which could mean selling off a home or two. Estate planning attorneys could be sources of very good referrals to this group of consumers.

We are right now living in the age of the greatest transfer of generational wealth. If the children of wealthy prospects are over 50 themselves, they are prime candidates for your services. We all know that there is usually a huge amount of money spent shortly after a large transfer of wealth. This makes the beneficiaries of fortunes a very good group to build relationships with. Again, estate planning professionals could be a great referral source for you.

Receivers of Wealth

The last group is comprised of retirees and divorced women. We are right now on the brink of the greatest number of people about to retire in history. That's about 33 million and counting. This is in addition to those that have already retired. I'm presently 61 and just on the far side of what are considered legitimate "baby boomers". While I'm not planning on retiring any time soon, you can bet the subject intrigues me more now than it did a decade ago.

There will also be retirees who are struggling financially, but there will also be a large segment of this group that are very comfortably set and would make excellent clients.

Then there are the ever-growing segment of divorced women. There are between 1.2 and 2.0 million divorces each year. When you have a couple divorcing whose income is in the top 5-10%, the wife will usually get to keep all of the liquid assets and the family home. The husband typically keeps the business-related assets.

No matter who keeps the family home, you know that some of the furnishings are going to go to the other spouse, so there will be a need for interior redesign services. And since the wife might also find herself without the amount of income she had become accustomed to receiving, she might start to feel a need to sell the home and perhaps even downsize.

So a divorced woman might be an excellent candidate for both staging and redesign services. You could position yourself as a stager or re-designer that caters specifically to the needs of a divorced person. Instead of trying to reach all women with your marketing message, why not focus instead on this special niche?

The Importance of Qualifying

Having established some of the areas and types of people who may be your best target market, or at least sources for referrals to your target market, I cannot emphasize enough the importance of qualifying each and every contact or prospect. You don't want to spin your wheels pitching your services to the wrong person. You must recognize that there is a difference between having great resources of income to invest with and having great sources of income.

Not every person with a great source of income has plenty of money to spend. They could be worth a lot of money, but actually be cash poor. If they are cash poor, they will be less receptive to your offers. So it is incumbent upon you to quickly detect who can easily afford your specialized services and who will turn a deaf ear or try to negotiate terms on the pricing.

Chapter 2
How Do the Affluent Think and Feel?

Focusing on the Luxury Client

As I said previously, the definition of "the affluent" may be different to different people, but to me it's the prospect or client who is considered by most standards to be wealthy - or at least wealthier than the average person in your area. So "being wealthy" is a relative term. Most

Americans are wealthy when compared to much of the world's population, particularly in third world countries

How you view wealthy people will be affected by your own personal income standard. There was a time in my life, when I was living paycheck to paycheck, and in the early days of being an entrepreneur, I would not have been able to write a book like this, because it's pretty hard to understand the mindset of those in the upper income brackets unless you're one of them. I'm certainly not in the category of top movie stars, professional athletes or some politicians. I live in a fairly large house in one of the most affluent counties in the nation, but I don't live in a multi-million dollar estate like some people. But I recognize that, by many people's standards, I am considered a wealthy person.

So in my own mind, I don't even consider myself to be necessarily among the affluent though others would. But in evaluating my own status and my evolving mindset and having served the upscale market to the degree I have, I can tell you that wealthy people think differently than the mainstream even though they have the same human nature as anyone else.

You see, human nature is the same all over the world. All mankind has the same basic needs and basic desires – to feel secure, to live comfortably, to take care of our families, to be able to dream and have hope of realizing our dreams. Human nature is the same today as it was at the dawn of creation. Human nature never changes. Even if our income level changes, our nature never does. So while you may or may not be an upscale consumer yourself, you will have the same nature of those that are.

Whether you are rich or poor or in between, you (and I) basically are only interested in what we feel will benefit us in some way. Think about it. Are you really interested in what benefits other people? Maybe a little, but what really peaks your interest is anything or anyone who has something to offer you that you believe will make life better for you in some way: something that will make you happier; something that will make you richer; something that will make life easier; something that will speed up a task, make you more comfortable, benefit your children, and be more pleasing to look at and so forth.

You don't have to be rich or poor to want to make life better for yourself and your family. So we all have that in common. That's human nature at work. It is how God made us and is a natural part of our makeup. However, we also know it can be perverted into a selfish obsession by some people.

Psyche of the Luxury Client

But just because human nature doesn't change, and just because we all share the same kind of human nature, that doesn't mean that all people in all income brackets think alike. They don't. We don't.

To illustrate what I mean, consider this. Low income people think about how they can get more money. High income people think about how they can make their money work for them more effectively so they can make even more money.

Low income people wonder about how they can get what they want even though they can't afford it. High income people think about how they can shelter their income from taxes. Low income people think that owning their own home is the epitome of success. High income people recognize that owning a home is a liability because it's not really making them income. Those, of course, aren't the only differences in the way the two groups think, but you get the point.

Having worked my way up the ladder of success over many years, I can assure you that I think differently now than when I was scraping by just to stay afloat. When I compare my life back then with my life today, my life today is definitely better. And I recognize that I am no longer the same person I was then, even though my nature hasn't changed.

I got annoyed at sales calls back then and they still annoy me today. I'm still careful about my money now as I was back then, though now I don't necessarily bother to look at price tags. But just as I weighed the value of something I was considering purchasing back then, I still weigh the value today. And while I can afford more now than back then, I'm still constantly evaluating value and worth.

One area of change in my thinking is that back when I was "poor" (at least by my perspective) I sought out discounts and sales so I could afford to buy something, hopefully without having to finance it. I didn't think much about sales people up-charging me because they probably didn't look upon me as an upscale customer.

Now that I'm in a higher income bracket, however, I'm more apt to be concerned about whether someone is elevating the price for goods and services for no other reason than that they think I can afford to pay more. I want to feel I got a good bargain just like anyone else. I don't want to be taken advantage of just because I make more money. I don't want to be up-charged any more than anyone else.

But I recognize that it's probably going to happen to me automatically. It's one of the reasons that I try not to be in any hurry when hiring a vendor to perform services for me. It's why I do my research and get bids. One should always do that no matter what one's income bracket, but I remain as diligent now as I ever have been because I still want to pay a fair price even though I can afford to pay a premium price.

So while I may find myself shopping in higher end stores now, I'm ever still looking for a sale or discount or bargain. That's human nature - and remember - human nature never changes.

Luxury Clients Are Not Naive

I just finished doing a redesign for an upscale client. Bill and Sally are young professionals, had just built a new multi-million dollar home on the water in Long Beach, CA. They did not inherit their wealth; they earned it over time. They demonstrated great taste, but needed help with accessorizing their home

The architect who built the home recommended an interior designer from Los Angeles to work with them on the interiors.

After pulling together a color board for the home and acquiring the major furniture pieces for their great room, Sally ultimately fired the guy. The reasons she gave me were: 1) She thought decorating her home should be a fun experience and he made it totally frustrating because he only wanted to do what suited his taste; 2) He charged her $10,000 to come from Los Angeles and provide her with one solitary vase.

Exasperated, Sally turned to the local university close by and contacted the interior design department. At this point she had additional furniture, lots of art and accessories that she wanted placed properly as she was hosting a fund-raising home tour in a month and wanted the home to look spectacular. All she needed was someone with skill to come and hang up her artwork and arrange her accessories.

The university had a design department and that is where Sally started searching for someone with design and decorating knowledge to come and work with her to complete the home, a 3-story Tuscan custom home of about 4,5000 square feet.

At last Sally found a gal who had just graduated with a degree in interior design and invited the lady to her home to see the scope of the project and give her a quote. The two did a walk through of the home and Sally showed the young designer what she had. The lady left and later submitted a quote of $40,000 to place Jan's accessories and hang her art.

Sally is not a cheap person by any stretch of the imagination, but she didn't have money to burn, having probably gone a bit over budget already in building the home. But whether she could afford the $40,000 or not, it seemed outrageously high to her. Shocking! Disappointing! I would definitely agree with her. What was the lady thinking? So Sally continued her search for the right person. A search on the internet brought her to my website and she called me up to discuss what I could do for her. We discussed the project and I quoted her the same full day price for redesign services that I give everyone. Sally was delighted. Not only was my fee completely affordable to her, but it felt fair to her and she could see that she was paying the same price anyone else would be paying, not one created just for her because of her income level nor based on my feelings about what she could afford. By the time I finished the project, which ultimately required two full days of redesign, Sally had paid substantially less for my services and was so happy she even gave me a $250 bonus.

Redesign for a Luxury Client

While I couldn't do everything Sally needed in one day, I think you'll find I made a major improvement in the way Sally's home looked, just in time for her tour. She wrote me after the tour and said the "home was a huge hit". She was thrilled with what I did for her and I was thrilled to have such a nice client, who immediately gave me a referral to some upscale friends and I'm in the process of finishing their home as I write this.

Sally also wrote that she personally handed my cards out to tour visitors all day long and assured me I should get more work coming my way. Whether I do or not, it is enough that Jan was so pleased with my services, and said so many times. Her husband was also very happy with the outcome, which is equally important to me.

The Stress of the Affluent

It is no secret that, for the most part, people who have built strong incomes are often small business owners, key corporate executives and top producing salespeople.

Anyone who is in a key position or who is responsible for the growth and management of a business (especially a large, successful business) knows full well that life can be, and usually is, stressful. In most business ventures, there is the matter of the overhead of the business, the matter of paying employees, the matter of advertising and promoting the business, the matter of research and development of new products and services, the fulfillment of the orders and customer care and service and on and on and on.

And even in the best run businesses, there is a level of stress that owners contend with that their employees will never quite understand. The demands on an owner's time, talent and energy are enormous and so these people quite naturally have a different point of view and a different set of motivators than other people have.

The Work Hours of the Affluent

Another one of the major factors that affect the life of the luxury, upscale consumer is that of time. Here is a break down of the work week of wealthy prospects and clients. When I said they are busy people, I said what I meant. You will find very, very few of them working less than 40 hours a week. It is not in their make-up. They tend to be very industrious people and will be hard to get a hold of. This is where persistence and tenacity are needed.

How do you measure up to them?

Hours Worked	Percentage
Over 60 hours a week	25.9%
From 50 to 60 hours	32.3%
From 40 to 50 hours	24.4%
40 hours or less	17.4%

If you really want to build a strong career in home staging and redesign, you must be prepared to work equally hard yourself. And it will be very good for you to show yourself as someone willing to do whatever is necessary to succeed. It is important for them to respect you too.

So it stands to reason that these people work long hours, usually more than 50 hours per week. Time, therefore, is at a premium, especially if they have families. Most do. Some of them might even have more than one stream of revenue: owning more than one business at a time, owning a business while also working for an employer.

So for these extremely busy people, time is of the essence. They don't have time to deal with tasks that they consider either boring or financially unproductive. They are, therefore, much less apt to be do-it-yourself stagers or decorators. They learned long ago to spend their quality time doing the things that advance their growing income and hiring people to do the tasks that would infringe on that.

This is why it is common for them to have housekeepers, gardeners, personal assistants, home stagers and re-designers. It would be foolish of them to spend time doing tasks that are typically handled by people willing to work for much less compensation than they earn.

So when approaching the affluent prospect, it would be well worth your while to really emphasize how much time you will save them and how much more lucrative it will be for them if they hire you to manage and troubleshoot the project on their behalf. Upscale consumers will really respond favorably to anything that saves them time and money and reduces the stress in their already overly busy life.

The Motivations of the Affluent

Think for a minute about your own buying habits and the things that motivate you to make a purchase, particularly a major purchase. While there are some differences in the motivations of the affluent compared to the non-affluent, there are also similarities.

When selling home staging and redesign services, you are a consultant, first and foremost. Because of that, anyone considering hiring you is in essence "buying you" as much as they are "buying your service".

First, affluent clients will evaluate your service based on the facts and data you supply them with. No surprises here. We all do that. Then they will evaluate you and how they feel about you. No surprises here either. We all do that.

But having weighed the data and facts, the benefits, they will not hire you until or unless they feel they can trust you. The buying decision will be an emotional response. They have to first feel comfortable about you and with you and feel they can trust you before they will decide to hire you.

The more influential they are, and the more affluent they are, the more they will need to trust you and believe that you have the expertise they require. So they will scrutinize the way you do business and the way you handle yourself.

Science is now discovering that people make decisions far more as an emotional response than ever believed to be true in the past. Let's face it. People buy homes because they fall in love with the home and can visualize themselves being happy in the home. They may start out with some special criteria for the home, but statistics prove that if they fall in love with the home, they are usually willing to adapt their criteria accordingly. They hire consultants the same way – starting with an emotional response to you and about you.

They want to hire someone who really knows what they are doing, and someone whom they believe will handle the project professionally with quality service. They don't have time or patience for anything but the best. So they will need to be convinced that you are capable of giving them the right advice at the right time. They won't tolerate mistakes very well.

So in the buying process, it starts with an emotional response to you. It then moves to an emotional conclusion about you. Then it eventually gets merged with whatever rational, non-emotional data they have been given to justify the decision that has been made.

Since they cannot take your service for a "test drive" or "try you out first", they will spend the entire time you are working on the project determining if they ultimately made the right decision.
This is why it is so vital that you perform in an outstanding manner throughout the staging or redesign process. You should leave no stone unturned. You should jump through hoops to service them and eliminate any and all hassles from their lives. You should, in the end, make doubly sure that everything has been done as promised, that you have over-delivered on your promises, that you have been professional in every sense of the word and given them the kind of follow up and service they deserve. Any failure along the way will cause them to second guess their original decision, and this will destroy any opportunity you might have to acquire on-going referrals.

Common Dissatisfaction Factors

Some of the most common themes for dissatisfaction among affluent clients include: 1) lack of value to justify the fees, commissions or charges for products; 2) a feeling that the consultant's advice is not in the best interest of the client; 3) a lack of sufficient information, facts and data for client to make an informed decision either before or during the process.

Later in this book I will deal with ways to overcome all of these obstacles to make sure that when you service an upscale client, you do not err before, during or after your project. I have found that many times a vendor working for me will do an adequate job before and during the project, but will fail at the tail end. And I always remember the lasting impression more than the first impression.

A few months ago my local phone company decided to add high speed capability throughout my neighborhood. While I don't mind them doing that at all, I'm quite unhappy about the way they left the neighborhood when they were done.

They came in unannounced to the neighborhood and dug up hundreds of holes in the streets and sidewalks. They jack hammered openings in the sidewalk in front of every home. I was one of the unlucky ones. When they uprooted the sidewalk, they also damaged the cement of a corner of my driveway.

To make matters worse, when they left, they did not clean up the area, leaving cement splatter all over the sidewalk, even on the street. They did not admit they had damaged my driveway and just left. That was 10 months ago and the pock-marked street has still not been resurfaced, so the entire neighborhood looks terrible.

I had no idea as to who was responsible for the mess until one day a repair truck was out front and I asked the men about it and they referred me to City Hall and said that it was the phone company's responsibility.

After 2 more months, the phone company finally sent a crew to clean off the cement splatter and they patched the driveway, but I'm not sure if the patching will hold up long term, so I'm still not a very happy camper. Who knows how long it will take for the city to come and put down a new surface on the street.

So do I have good thoughts about the phone company? Not any more. By the way, my home is the only home in the neighborhood that wound up with such a mess. The workmen had obviously gathered up their tools and left, making no effort whatsoever to leave the area clean and without any problems.

First impressions get you the job. But it is the lasting impressions that get you referrals or not. And the experience as a whole is what your client will talk about to other people, which can help you or hurt you.

Chapter 3
Where to Find the Affluent

The Geographic Distribution

There are, of course, millionaires all over the place. But here in the United States, there are some states that have a higher number of wealthy prospects than other states.

Leading the pack is California, New York and Texas, as you might expect.

In the northeast, the leaders after the big 3 above are: New Jersey, Pennsylvania and Massachusetts. In the southeast, you have Florida, Virginia and Maryland. In the Great Lakes area you'll find Illinois, Michigan, and Ohio. And in the west, a good number of millionaires live in California, Washington and Arizona.

There are millionaires in the other states as well, but the numbers drop quite a bit comparatively speaking.

Gathering Places of the Affluent

So the question is, "Where do the affluent go between 8:00 am and 6:00 pm on a weekday?" They usually work somewhere other than where they live. The highest number of them probably can be found at or near the Wall Street District of Manhattan Island. And whether it be on Wall Street or some other street inhabited by the rich, they do tend to cluster together. You can find whole buildings filled with highly successful corporate types and sales professionals.

When I was actively working as a corporate art consultant, my associate and I would canvass entire buildings of white collar companies, starting at the top of the building and working our way down. You start at the top because the most successful companies are located on the top floors. We never, ever ran into anyone else canvassing the building. Some clever entrepreneurs have sought out affluent prospects for car pooling or for seat selection on commuter trains and buses. There are no secretaries to screen out your calls and your conversations will be largely uninterrupted. And you're likely to have zero competition.

There are also affluent neighborhoods. Don't judge a neighborhood by the cars. But you can get a feeling for the caliber of ownership by the caliber of the residence. Houses on a bluff overlooking the ocean are a pretty safe bet to be owned by wealthy prospects.

Check out affluent business communities and industrial parks. More difficult to do, but you could cold call on entrepreneurs where they work. In many industrial areas you'll find dozens of affluent business owners all within a few acres of one another.

You won't often find the wealthy at home. They are very busy and active if they are business owners, executives and sales professionals who are not retired yet. They will likely be at the top of their chosen field. One of the reasons they are at the top is because they continually keep themselves well informed about their industry, the changes in the market for what they sell, their competition and so forth. I'll say it again: Small businesses produce more millionaires in America than any other segment of the economy. But to find these people, you have to find at work – which is where they are most of the time.

How do they keep themselves so well informed? By attending conferences on an international, national, regional, state and local level – that's how. Read on.

Trade Conferences

Check to see if you have a local chapter of the <u>Sales and Marketing Executives</u> (SME) in your neck of the woods. SME is a professional organization for senior sales and marketing managers and executives. If you want to find a concentration of affluent individuals to network among, don't forget the fortunes being amassed by sales professionals from every conceivable industry. Another interesting tidbit is that sales people are among some of the easiest people in the world to convince. It is common knowledge that sales professionals, by their own admission, are very susceptible to sales pitches.

So if you are offering a home staging business, should you be attending and networking at conferences for the real estate industry? You bet. And if you are doing interior redesign, should you be attending conferences in the interior design industry? You bet.

How about conferences for the moving industry, the furniture industry, the accessory industry, the home improvement industry? Or how about the conferences for the industry for which your geographic location is famous? Silicon Valley in California is famous for the computer science industry. Perhaps you're in farm country. There are a lot of rich farmers out there. Or perhaps you are in the heart of the automobile industry or surrounded by grape vineyards. Wherever you live, look around you. There are luxury clients everywhere. You just have to locate them locally and target them specifically.

Industry Trade News and Magazines

Subscribe to the industry trade news and magazines of the industries you want to target. Get to know the major players. Learn about the industry, it's problems, it's growth. Man a booth at one of their conferences.

Look for businesses up for sale and listed in trade association publications. Why businesses for sale? Because whenever that business does sale, that owner is going to come into a lot of money and there will be a bright window of opportunity for you whenever there is a transfer of a large amount of money.

By starting to build a relationship with that prospect before the business sells, you will be in a prime position to offer your staging and redesign services at the appropriate time. Many, many people, upon getting a large amount of money all at one time look to upgrade their residence by buying up, or by investing in more property. But without a prior existing relationship, your ability to land a project diminishes.

You aren't likely to have any competition either, because how many stagers and re-designers will be researching and working to develop a long lasting relationship with this person? You'll probably be the only one.

Home Builders for Luxury Clients

Pulte Homes is one home builder who has come to recognize the importance of staging properties for quick sale. One savvy stager has already set herself up as the official Pulte Home Stager in her area. The company offers her services to buyers who already own a home and need to sell it in order to buy a Pulte home. They pay the stager to provide the basic consultation. Any additional services the stager may do are negotiated between the stager and the homeowner.

This is good business of Pulte Homes, their home buyers and the stager.

Now if one home builder can see the benefit to working with an independent stager, the other home builders can't be far behind. Those that get in early on this ripe area to work will reap the rewards and pretty much lock up the opportunities in their area.

So find out whose building homes in your area. Contact the builder. Put together a proposal that is benefit driven for them and for their buyers and you could wind up with a beautiful on-going opportunity for yourself.

Be prepared to offer your services at a slight discount in exchange for the automatic referrals you will get. That's only fair.

Property Management Companies

Property management companies work with people in transition. People in transition are buying and selling homes. People in transition are moving furnishings from one location into a new location. People in transition are prime candidates for staging and redesign services.

Property management companies know in advance who is moving and often know other important details of the status and timing of these movements. Therefore they can be great sources for referrals. By alerting you to the transition and timing of their clients, you can begin building a relationship with these people early enough to pay off for you when the actual move takes place.

If approached correctly, a good property management executive or sales professional can be a great source of timely information for you.

Insider Information

Two of your best sources of information on the transfer of wealth can come from attorneys and CPAs. They work closely with people who need legal and financial help to manage their affairs, which would include the sale of property, the sale of businesses, pending or post inheritances, the distribution of wealth to heirs and so forth. As I stated earlier, one of the best times to approach anyone with a service or product for sale is right after they have received a large sum of money.

There is a brief time of euphoria when spending increases. By being alerted of such transfers of wealth from an attorney or CPA who trusts you, you are in a prime position to approach an affluent prospect at just the right time.

Funeral Parlor Directors

Funeral parlors and obituary columns are also great resources in learning about the transfer of wealth in your area. Obituary columns will tell you the names of the heirs even. Building a trusting relationship with a funeral parlor director can also be beneficial. Of course, due to the timing of events relating to the death of someone, you need to obviously be sensitive to those who are grieving in general, but specifically to anyone benefiting financially as a result of the death.

Also, people who inherit or are benefactors of a large sum of money may not have been affluent prior to the death of a loved one, but become affluent upon the transfer of the inheritance. Use this research data with respect and a great deal of tact.

Chapter 4
Networking with the Affluent

How and Where to Meet Well-to-do Women or Couples

Let's face it: women rule the home. If you want to get anywhere in the home staging or interior redesign business, you've got to connect with the woman. Few men care that much, although they do care about turning a higher profit upon selling a home. But when it comes to decorating a home, you're almost always going to need to convince the woman that your services are needed.

You have to go where the rich and soon-to-be-rich spend their time. Many **yacht clubs** allow people to join on social status who don't even own boats. What better way to meet a well-to-do woman or couple than to be a member of this club and be present at the various social functions the club provides? This allows you to mingle with a lot of people of means. A couple of good "reasons" for joining would be to take sailing lessons if offered, or to be researching for inside tips for purchasing a boat.

If you're a horse lover, find an exclusive stable or **riding club** and join up. This doesn't mean you have to have a horse of your own to learn to ride. If the club has gatherings for all the members, it's an excellent opportunity to make friends with upscale members.

Better supermarkets are excellent meeting places for the upwardly mobile, as are better department stores. You can be working there or shopping there, it's just more difficult to actually strike up a conversation in that setting. Some of the really large stores such as Bloomingdales in New York have entire departments devoted to party needs such as wine, cheese, crackers or hors d'oeuvres, etc. Want to meet a nice on-the-way up type of woman (or couple), this may be a fun place to get a friendship started. It's a sure bet if you're looking around this type of party center, a conversation may develop if you let it or even better, start it.

In University towns, the **libraries** are excellent meeting places for soon to be lawyers and doctors and other assorted professional types. I'm referring to the University library as opposed to the public one. This could necessitate enrolling in one course to get the card entitling you to use the library. Take something fun and easy – or, for a novel idea, take something educational.

 Then there are your local **Golf Clubs**. Now there are probably more men who golf than women, but sometimes it can be advantageous to meet the husband first and let him introduce you to the wife. Here is where some of our great **Musical Slideshow CDs** (see Chapter 13) can come in handy. You can place one in the husband's hand and ask him to take it home to show the wife. You make a pre-appointment to pick it up at the home, and you turn the prospect into a paid client, just like that! You can also take lessons, no matter what level you are at as a golfer, or if you've never played, join a beginner's class.

Then there's the good old **Tennis Club**. Lots of upscale couples enjoy playing tennis together. Even if they don't play, it's kind of an elite status thing to belong to a tennis club. It conjures up visions of people sitting around the courts in their white shorts and shirts, sipping drinks and enjoying good conversation. Again, you don't have to know how to play tennis. But it helps to know how to meet people and enter into light conversation. As with golf and boating, lessons are a good way to get into the dynamics of being a member.

Setting up a table or booth at a **Job Fair** is a great way to inform and education your community about your profession as a home stager or re-designer. This also gives you opportunities to find employees or an apprentice for your business as it grows.

Many communities have **Newcomers Clubs**. Join one as a volunteer. You'll be privy to all of the new residents moving into your community. You may be one of those who go out to bring a packet of materials to the new homeowner. If you can't be the one distributing the literature, at least try to get a business card or postcard included in the packet. When a person first moves into a new space, that's the time when they are most apt to be interested in a redesign service, because you'll be able to help them make their old furnishings work in the new space.

Join your local **Chamber of Commerce**. You'd be surprised how many prominent men and women are part of this organization. Not only will you find successful business people attending, but you'll also find politicians who attend. All of these types of people fall into the upscale target market. If you want to connect with them, you have to go where they go. And join with the right attitude. Join to contribute, not just glean. Be a giver, not merely a taker. Over time, you'll find a lot of business can come from such a group and the referrals they will generate for you.

Join the **Booster Clubs** for your local high schools. Help them raise money for the school programs. There are booster clubs for athletics, cheerleading, debate teams and so forth. Consider giving a yearly scholarship to a graduating senior who wants to attend college and study interior design. This will get your name circulating among students and their parents.

Look for other **Fund Raising Groups** to join. One of my upscale clients belongs to a fundraising group for a local hospital. People who join fund raising effort are usually people with money who donate to these same causes. Become a volunteer to help the group. A natural by-product of your membership will be the friendships you make with the other fund raisers. You'll be helping a worthy cause in addition to promoting your services.

Ask at your library to see if they have any **Book Clubs**. Upscale women who don't work have the time to become avid readers, which can result in them joining book clubs. I mean, what else are they going to do with their extra time while their husband is at work? Perhaps there will be a club that will focus on topics that include decorating the home. Again, I emphasize the importance of participation and contribution. Give and it will be given to you.

If you are an alumni from your local high school, community college or university, be sure to join their **Alumni Club**. Not only do alumni tend to stick together because of a natural common bond, but you'll meet people from many different graduating years. This can be both fascinating and financially rewarding. Focus on the baby boomers, however, because they are the people who have grown their incomes, grown their children and now have expendable cash with which to hire you.

Become a volunteer in your favorite **Political Organization**. They are always in need of help and again you'll have a common philosophical bond with other volunteers. This may in time put you in contact with some pretty important people in your local region. It never hurts to make friends with powerful people.

Affluent Referral Networks

One of the best ways to join in social contact with upscale potential clients is to join the same types of clubs, associations and organizations they frequent. And by joining, I don't mean showing up periodically. I mean becoming a vibrant part of the group, even a leader, if you can. You will then have the most visibility and, over time, should find yourself making many friendships that can turn into a client/designer/stager/art consultant relationship.

Networking in General

The American Bar Association

The American Bar Association, with hundreds of thousands of members, attorneys and judges, meets every August. There is a disproportionate share of wealthy prospects in the legal profession. Law partnership revenue is in the billions of dollars. It is a huge and very lucrative industry.

And who do these attorneys and judges like to associate with? Well, other attorneys and judges. One of my favorite redesigns was for a Superior Court Judge in Los Angeles. His house is in the suburbs and he commutes daily to the court. Every week he and a handful of other judges, who form a small private band, get together in his living room to make music. They aren't professional musicians. They just like to "jam".

The American Bar Association's official website is www.abanet.org. You can find help locating an attorney, check out the attorney resources and even contact their member services for specifics on industry magazines and publications. Why not position yourself as a home stager or re-designer who specializes in the needs of attorneys and judges? Submit articles for publication, sponsor events, try to get speaking engagements at local chapters.

Encyclopedia of Associations

Below I'm giving you an extensive list of organizations that cater to women. The reason for this is that the vast majority of stagers and re-designers who purchase this training are women. However, if you want to target associations and organizations in general, you should pick up a copy of the *Encyclopedia of Associations,* published by Gale Research Company of Detroit. You'll find important details on the key trade association of various industries. They will give you the size of membership, the location and dates of annual conventions, the publications these members tend to subscribe to and a list of the major players in the industry.

Networking with Women

Advancing Women -- This International Network for Women in the Workplace highlights issues for the working woman. Includes an online career center, Today's Women's News feature, forums for discussion, links for networking with international women, personal services resources and links to similar sites. E-mail: publisher@advancingwomen.com

BellaOnline -- Online resource for women that has career and networking advice, as well as chat areas and discussion forums for online networking.

DinnerGirls.org -- a great networking and mentoring site for women, from all over the world. Includes both online resources and network, as well as local chapters in some U.S. cities. For all women, from college student to CEO.

iVillage.com -- Another online women's resource with career and networking advice, and chat areas and message boards for online networking.

Business Women's Network (BWN) -- Is dedicated to the promotion of business and professional women by providing assistance to corporations, businesswomen's organizations and state and federal agencies. BWN strives to be the authority on issues affecting businesswomen and the growth of women-owned businesses. Offers searchable online business women's network directory.

Women's Professional Organizations:

Selected women's professional organizations are provided here.

American Association of University Women (AAUW)
1111 16th St., NW
Washington, DC 20036
Phone: 202-785-7700
Email: info@aauw.org
This is a national organization that promotes education and equity for all women and girls. As college graduates, they are bound to make good income in their respective careers.

American Business Women's Association (ABWA)
9100 Ward Pkwy.
Kansas City, MO 64114-0728
Phone: 816-361-6621
Email: abwa@abwa.org
These members are entrepreneurs. They will be busy but probably command high incomes. Call the ABWA's national headquarters to make contact with their local organization and members.

American Medical Women's Association
Suite 400, 801 N. Fairfax St.
Alexandria, VA 22314
Phone: 703-838-0500
Email: info@amwa-doc.org
This group will put you in touch with women doctors, nurses and other health care professionals.

American Woman's Society of Certified Public Accountants (AWSCPA)
401 N. Michigan Avenue
Chicago, Illinois 60611
Phone: 312-664-6610, 800-AWSCPA-1
FAX: 312-527-6783
Email: admin@awscpa.org
To network among women CPAs who can be great mentors and sources of referrals, this is an ideal group. You can even find info on their website about networking opportunities.

Association for Women in Communications
c/o Suite 301, 1733 20th St., NW

Washington, DC 20009
Phone: 202-973-2136
Offers a mentor program and an annual career day.

Association for Women in Computing
Suite 1006, 41 Sutter St.
San Francisco, CA, 94104
Phone: 415-905-4663
Email: info@awc-hq.org
Serves programmers, analysts, technical writers, and entrepreneurs. Many fortunes are being amassed by people using the internet. You might even network your way into a nice website design.

Association for Women in Development (AWID)
Suite 825, 1511 K St., NW
Washington, DC 20005
Phone: 202-628-0440
Email: awid@awid.org
While maybe a more difficult industry group, international groups may not have any competition going after their business. This group serves women working on international-development issues.

American Women in Radio and Television (AWRT)
Suite 200, 1650 Tysons Blvd.
McLean, VA 22102
Phone: 703-506-3290
Email: info@awrt.org
Serves women working in electronic media and related fields and might be a great resource to reach into the entertainment industries too.

Association for Women in Science (AWIS)
Suite 650, 1200 New York Ave., NW
Washington, DC 20005
Phone: 202-326-8940; 800-886-AWIS
Email: awis@awis.org
Here is another association meeting the needs women in science, mathematics, engineering, and technology. AWIS has more than 5,000 members. They have 76 chapters all over the country.

Association of Women in International Trade (WIIT)
PO Box 65962
Washington, DC 20035
Phone: 202-785-9842
Another strong organization dealing in international industry and

probably an untapped organization for staging and re-design.

Business and Professional Women USA
1900 M Street NW, Suite 310
Washington, DC 20036
Phone: 202-293-1100
Focused on more general issues of interest to women, this group is made of women who are professional and likely to respect other professional women.

Commercial Real Estate Women (CREW)
1201 Wakarusa Dr., Ste. C3
Lawrence, KS 66049
Phone: 785-832-1808
For women working in all facets of commercial real estate. While their focus is commercial real estate, these women could become great mentors and sources for referrals.

Financial Women International (FWI)
Suite 814, 200 N. Glebe Rd.
Arlington, VA 22203-3128
Phone: 703-807-2007
Email: info@fwi.org
Formerly known as the National Association of Bank Women, FWI is for women in banking services. Banks are sources for new loans to buyers and property in transition.

Federally Employed Women (FEW)
Suite 425, 1400 I St., NW
Washington, DC 20005-2252
Phone: 202-898-0994
Email: few@few.org
Serves women in all levels of the federal government, including the military. Military people are often in transition and need of staging services. When someone gets transferred, they usually need to take steps to sell a home in a short amount of time.

International Alliance for Women in Music (IAWM)
Department of Music
George Washington University, NW
Washington, DC 20052
Phone: 202-994-6338
Serves composers, conductors, performers, and music lovers. If you have musical talents, you could easily bond with members of this group

and even specialize in serving musicians of all genres of music, including teachers as well as performers.

National Association for Female Executives (NAFE)
60 East 42nd St., Suite 2700
New York, NY 10165
Phone: 212-351-6400
Email: nafe@nafe.com
This is the largest women's association and is nationwide. Using education and networking it helps its members achieve career success.

National Association of Insurance Women
1847 E. 15th St.
Tulsa, OK 74104
Phone: 800-766-NAIW
Email: National@naiw.org
Provides opportunities for women in the insurance industry. Insurance sales people have inside data on the income of their clients and are also a great target market themselves.

National Association of Women Business Owners
Suite 1100, 1511 K St., NW
Washington, DC 20005
Phone: 202-638-5322
When you've had your business for eight or more years, you'll qualify to join this organization. Chances are the members of this group are now affluent members and a great target market to specialize in.

National Coalition of 100 Black Women, Inc.
38 West 32nd Street, Suite 1610
New York, NY 10001-3816
Phone: 212-947-2196
Email: nc100bw@aol.com
This nonprofit organization made of volunteers focused on community service, leadership development and career enhancement. Great networking opportunities and a more neglected target market.

National Women's Political Caucus
Suite 425, 1211 Connecticut Ave., NW
Washington, DC 20036
Phone: 202-785-1100
Women in politics. They often go on to make very good incomes and become influential people. Another great group to network among.

Society of Women Engineers
120 Wall St.
New York, NY 10005
Phone: 212-509-9577
Engineers are highly detailed people who love lots of data. If you're the kind that loves to talk about facts and figures, this is the group for you.

Women in Advertising and Marketing
4200 Wisconsin Ave., NW
Washington, DC 20016
Phone: 301-369-7400
Joining a group like this will also teach you much about how to market your services.

Women in Housing and Finance (WHF)
6712 Fisher Ave.
Falls Church VA 22046
Phone: 703-536-5112
Email: whf@whfdc.org
With interests in insurance, securities and technology, this group is bound to be affluent and very knowledgeable on housing issues. They could be great resource for home stagers.

Women in International Security (WIIS)
Center for Peace and Security Studies
Edmund A. Walsh School of Foreign Service
Georgetown University
Washington, DC 20005-1145
Phone: 202-687-3366
Email: info@wiis.org
Dedicated to enhancing opportunities for women in foreign and defense policy. How many stagers and re-designers would go after a group of women like this? Probably not one. You got to think outside the box.

Women in Technology International (WITI)
12015 Lee-Jackson Hwy.
Fairfax, VA 22033
Phone: 703-267-3565
Interested in all aspects of technology, this group is probably not very good with decorating their homes. A ripe opportunity to gain some great clients who can afford your services.

Women's Caucus for the Arts (WCA)

PO Box 1498, Canal St. Station
New York, NY 10013
Phone: 212-634-0007
Anyone in the arts is a prime candidate for your services and for referrals to other people in the arts. As creative people themselves, they should understand the emotional impact of a beautiful home.

Women's Information Network (WIN)
Suite 635, 1511 K St., NW
Washington, DC 20005
Phone: 202-347-2827
High-level professional women share their experiences at informal dinner parties with younger women. No matter which side of the age spectrum you are on, this could be a profitable group to network with.

Mentoring Services

A great way to attract the luxury client is to present your self as their personal mentor. To be a successful mentor, you must have the best interest of your client foremost in your mind. You must successfully convey that attitude in everything you do and say. This is not always easy to do if your advice to them means not closing a sale or taking less profit than you would like.

It takes a warm hearted, self-sacrificing, genuinely honest person to use the mentoring process as a major means of growing a business. If your back is against the wall financially, you will find it much more difficult to be a quality mentor than if you have plenty of work and plenty of profit coming in.

When prospective trainees call me up to get more information about my courses and training options or to get advice from me on what route is best for them, I genuinely try hard to steer them in the direction that is best for them.

One of the first questions I will ask is, "What are your goals?" If they answer that they are looking for supplemental income, I never recommend they become a Gold or Diamond trainee. That probably would not be in their best interest.

Recently a man wrote me inquiring about my Diamond course. He wanted me to give him a payment plan. He told me that he just spent 2 years bedridden and suffers from multiple sclerosis.

I don't know if he was telling me the truth or not, but I advised him not to buy the Diamond program and to start out with the basic training tutorial instead. I questioned his ability to do a home staging business with his physical limitations.

He took my advice and purchased the electronic book. A couple of weeks later he wrote and asked for a refund because he quickly determined that, indeed, he was not physically capable of doing this type of work.

I probably could have gotten him to invest in the non-refundable Diamond course if I had tried. But I practice what I preach. I whole heartedly did not believe he should go down that path, and I'm very happy that, in the end, I conducted myself in an honorable manner, advising him on what was best for him.

You can never go wrong focusing on the best interests of your client, but you have to be dedicated to that position. Had he purchased the course as he originally wanted, and then wrote me for a refund, I would not have been able to accommodate the request. It is against company policy and I don't do for one trainee what I don't do for all trainees. So it was a good thing he wrote me first before plunking down his money.

You might think that wealthy people don't need advice. Nothing could be further from the truth. They may be at the top of their game in their industry, but might not know much about yours.

A multi-million dollar client of mine, living on the shore in Long Beach, was a tremendously successful marketer and manager in the rental car industry. He was the regional director for one of the largest groups within his company, now the world's largest rental car agency.

But he didn't know the first thing about interior design. So most of the time when we were together, it was me who talked from a position of expertise and knowledge, not him. Over the years of our business relationship, I had multiple opportunities to steer him in a better direction than he had planned to go. He really trusted my advice. And I was able to make a lot of money as a result, not just from serving him and his company, but from serving his friends and associates as well.

Real Estate Adviser

If you are a real estate agent or broker, you can present yourself to potential prospects as an expert in all phases of real estate, not just home staging or redesign.

If you are offering multiple services to a client, it's difficult to know which one to pitch to them and it's not that good of an idea to throw everything at them all at once. So you would be especially advised to put your prospects on a mailing list or email list and send them advice on a wide number of topics related to home ownership, buying and selling, staging and redesign, finance and so forth. This way you present yourself as their adviser, not just a home stager or re-designer. By writing to them on some sort of planned schedule, you continually remind them that you are there ready to help them and advise them, and they learn to trust you and see you as an expert, not as a salesperson.

To be the most effective, you should use a soft sell approach, mainly focusing on free information to help them now or in the future, and casually focusing on the benefits of hiring you for services.

Finder's Fees and Commissions

As you find yourself in situations where you can benefit a real estate agent, it's a good idea to form a business agreement with regards to finder's fees or commissions. Many agents will be happy to give you one and even have established their own set of fees for this purpose. Some may want to base the fee on a percentage of their commissions and others will prefer a flat fee. Try to place yourself in a reciprocal position at the very least whereby they are helping you build your business in exchange for you helping them. Before you approach any agent, it's good to get a feel for what is typical in your community. You can do this by simply calling a selection of agents, perhaps slightly out of your area, and inquiring about their finder's fees. When you know the going rate in your area, then you'll know exactly what is fair to request.

Think about it. How cool would it be to work with an affluent homeowner before the house is put on the market – before they have hired an agent? How cool would it be to hook up the homeowner with an agent you have relationship with, and work a deal in advance with the agent to get 1% of the agent's commission as your finder's fee (or whatever is standard for your area) for hooking the two of them up?

Or how beneficial would it be to cut a deal with the homeowner for that 1% prior to staging the home at all? It's being done! 1% of a $500,000 home is $5,000. 1% of a $1,000,000 home is $10,000. 1% of a $5,000,000 estate is $50,000. Could you use that money wisely?

Before you even contemplate such agreements, make sure all agreements are in writing, signed by all parties and dated and handled in escrow. See an attorney to draw up your generic agreement.

Talent Scout

Since a huge number of affluent prospects own their own businesses, that means that they are in constant need of quality suppliers of products and services. While giving out referrals and recommendations can be risky, it is a way to build relationships.

The affluent need advice in many areas, not only for their business, but for the home and family as well. So having a list of truly good professionals in a wide range of services could be quite advantageous to you.

This list could include such professionals as: attorneys, CPAs, movers, plant services, financial planners, stock brokers, florists, carpet cleaners, electricians, plumbers, painters, wallpaper hangers, carpet installers, window replacement companies, landscapers, gardeners, carpenters, furniture makers, and on and on. You get the point.

Add to this list leaders in such fields as advertising, estate planning, commercial real estate, marketing, public relations, production management and materials procurement. You don't have to offer a commercial product or service to be able to give referrals in these important areas to the entrepreneurs you wish to attract.

Now read this carefully. Your top focus as a talent scout is to locate prospects who are centers of influence. It doesn't help you all that much if you're working hard to hook up people who can't reciprocate in any way that will benefit you. It's a nice thing to do, but don't confuse just being nice with being a smart talent scout. Smart talent scouts reserve their best efforts to helping those people who can help them in return beyond the average person.

So don't spin your wheels. You need to focus your energies on people who influence a large number of other affluent prospects. Like why not try to become a talent scout for the president of an affluent trade association? That person is in a position to influence hundreds, maybe even thousands of affluent prospects on your behalf.

When you have gone out of your way to put your prospect or client in touch with a professional that can help them in some related or even non-related area, your prospect/client will have a feeling or sense of obligation to you to reciprocate in some manner. Their appreciation of your efforts on their behalf can lead to endorsements of you and your services. It's always good for your business to have some affluent consumers feel indebted to you in some way.

Publicist

Do you have a marketing or public relations background who needed to get into your own business and become independent. Don't just use that expertise to market your business. Use it to offer to help the wealthy entrepreneur you're trying to attract to market HIS/HER business. Look for ways to pass along ideas for consideration that will help your prospect make money or save money with their business. Point out that by using one of your ideas, they might make enough new profit to completely cover the costs associated with hiring you as a stager or re-designer.

Use the contacts you already have to benefit the entrepreneur and you will be perceived in a whole different light. You might even get a job offer – not that you're looking for one. But when you generously help people out, even if it is in an unrelated field, you'd be amazed at how generous and helpful they can be in return.

Income Enhancer

An income enhancer is similar to a talent scout, except that this person looks for ways to make the client more money as a conscious act. Obviously in home staging, that is the goal. A good home stager will strive to not only make the client more money in the sale of the property, but speed up the process too.

As a revenue enhancer, you'll want to ask your prospect or client, "What is your top need – your number one need in your business?" Most entrepreneurs will answer, "To make more money."

There are certain core products and services that a home stager or re-designer tends to offer. But don't you think it would be smart to offer more than the core products and services? I mean, all things being equal, don't you think a savvy prospect would lean more heavily toward hiring the company or person that offered a wider service or more products than the competitor?

Wouldn't it be great to have prospects seek you out? Wouldn't it be great to have prospects go out of their way to refer business to you? You can create your own demand by offering home owners and real estate agents additional products or services that meet a wider need they share in common.

The more you can separate your products and services from the norm, the more you will carve out a reputation that is hard to match or beat.

If you could substantially help your client make more money in a separate business owned by the client, don't you think you would bond yourself to that client forever and be in a position to receive a lot of referrals?

Can you see the value of hooking up your client/prospect with connections above and beyond staging or redesign needs?

What if you subscribed to some industry publications in your prospect's field. What if you interviewed suppliers of your client's industry and helped to narrow down the field of suppliers, pricing, service and then passed that information along to your prospect/client. Do you think that would help you establish a deeper bond with your prospect making it almost unthinkable for your client to consider doing business with anyone but you?

What do you think would be the reaction to you if you made a habit of saying to every prospect or client, *"Give me a supply of your business cards. I just may have many clients or business contacts who are likely to buy from you."*

How would you feel as an entrepreneur yourself if someone you were contemplating doing business with asked you that question. All of us want to make more money, I wager. All of us would respond very favorably to anyone willing to help us achieve that goal, particularly if that help came free of charge with no string attached.

Believe me, the average home stager and the average interior re-designer are not asking that question and are not practicing the art of being an income enhancer on behalf of their prospect/client.

Loan Broker

Since credit is one of the most essential needs that anyone has in their business and personal life, assisting a prospect/client to acquire credit or to businesses or individuals who are experts in acquiring credit or repairing credit could enhance your business over time.

When I say "repair credit", I'm not talking about referring a client or prospect to a company that promises to clean up their credit for them at a fee. Most such companies are shams and are duping the public.

But I am talking about tips and suggestions that a person or business might be privy about that would help the client or prospect to do what is necessary to minimize damage or negative dings to their own credit report.

So you could, as one of your non-core products or services, help a prospect or client attain a loan at a better than average rate, maybe even negotiating a loan with better origination fees as well. If you are good at negotiating and networking, you just might find that by adding this type of service to your list will separate you from your competitors and help you brand your business in an unusual way.

By helping your prospect/client to find ways to attain a loan, you not only have helped them achieve something valuable, but you have creatively caused the transfer of a large sum of money at one time, thus bringing about the perfect timing for closing a sale yourself in your core service of being a home stager or interior re-designer.

I hope by now you're beginning to understand the value of helping your prospect/client in ways that might not directly be connected with your core business. Whether your client/prospect is an entrepreneur or a wage earner or a commissioned salesperson, he/she has relationships with other businesses or individuals that could be valuable clients for you.

So the referral potential and the networking possibilities could be staggering. I don't care if a referral comes to me for help in an out of the ordinary manner or not – so long as the referral comes to me. How often have you contacted a business or individual about one matter and wound up hiring that person for something quite different than you thought you would do? It happens to us all.

You will even find buyers of real estate setting out to purchase a home with a definite set of criteria who change their requirements after falling in love with a house. So it should come as no surprise when a client changes the criteria along the way when it comes to hiring you for a project.

It is not inconceivable to work on a home staging project and do such a fine job that your client decides to keep the home rather than sell it because they have fallen in love with the home all over again. What a nice compliment for you if it happens and what a great referral opportunity too.

Realtors Who Also Stage

If you are already a real estate agent or broker, then you have a decided advantage over those people who become home stagers or re-designers but who do not have a real estate license.

You're going to be privy to insider information, marketing skill sets and so forth in your training that will benefit you greatly. Just the contacts alone that you will probably already have in place will be highly valuable.

If you're not an agent already, you might even consider getting your real estate license. Do I consider this a conflict of interest? Not at all. Being a home stager/re-designer and an agent gives you the best of both worlds.

The real estate business is a regulated industry, however, and you will have to get your real estate license before you can hang out your shingle. But that is not horribly difficult to achieve. There are courses you can take, seminars you can attend and so forth that can help you achieve that goal. Companies exist whose sole purpose is to train you on how to get your license.

By becoming a licensed real estate agent, you will not only gain more credibility as a home stager, but you will look far more attractive to prospects if you are a licensed agent than if you are not. You don't have to go get your license, but it can only help you if you do.

Advocate

Have you ever stopped to think that affluent people are often connected with events such as charity, fund raising or education based? In fact many upscale clients complain that there are just too few professionals that have demonstrated any interest in supporting the causes that they are interested in.

Years ago I began an investment strategy by taking out a whole life insurance policy that would pay out dividends. Over time those dividends would mound up significantly. I'm talking quite significantly over the course of a lifetime of investing.
My financial consultant was a member of my own family who had never really cared about having a close relationship with me. He was more of a loner and I knew from the outset that he wasn't very interested in my prosperity. But he was "family" so I chose to build my portfolio through his company.

Being well trained by his company to build a relationship with clients, he started calling me periodically and about once a year he invited me out to lunch, where he pretended to be interested in me.

Unknown to him, I was always evaluating him quietly. His lack of genuineness would surface, not at lunch, but over the phone. He was going through some rough waters from time to time with his relationship with his wife. He would call me up and tell me all about their troubles.

Being someone who wanted to be of help, I would listen for hours to his problems and give him advice which he swore he would take but rarely did. And invariably, like clock work, in the hundred or so conversations I had with him over the phone, he never tired of talking about himself. He would rehash the same old things for hours at a time.

But just as predictable as he was in revisiting all of his problems, he was predictable when it came to discussing any topic not centered on him. To put it bluntly, whenever the conversation veered off onto me or my family, he suddenly had to hang up.

And since our phone calls were toll calls, he couldn't hang up fast enough if he was paying for the call.

I never ever said anything to him about his selfish behavior, but I was never fooled into thinking he cared about me as a client and he got no referrals from me ever over the years I was investing through him.

Don't put yourself out there as an advocate, someone who cares about what is best for your prospect or client, if you're secretly focused only on what's in it for you. You will be found out, I guarantee it. And you probably will never know why you got dumped or never got a referral.

Life has a way of making everything transparent – in time.

If you do genuinely care about the needs of your prospect or client, then you will probably try to find ways to help them out – without being asked to do so. By talking to your client about their business and personal lives, you'll gain a lot of information that could be used to help them out. You'll find out about what they care about beyond the home or beyond selling the home.

So let's say, for example, that you found out that your client was having trouble with becoming compliant with some housing regulation (perhaps a gated community regulation or condo requirement or some city ordinance of some kind), or you found out that your client's industry was facing some hardship or unfair treatment. And let's say you took the time to write a letter to the editor of your local newspaper or magazine.

Let's say your letter to the editor gets published because you're pointing out a specific problem that your client is facing and that others might be facing as well. Then you clip out the letter from the newspaper, and you send a copy of it to all of the leading executives in your client's industry, pointing out to them your reasons for writing the letter in the first place.

What if you sent a note along with the copy of the newspaper and it said something like?

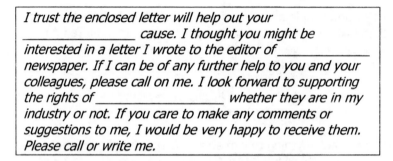

I trust the enclosed letter will help out your _____ cause. I thought you might be interested in a letter I wrote to the editor of _____ newspaper. If I can be of any further help to you and your colleagues, please call on me. I look forward to supporting the rights of _____ whether they are in my industry or not. If you care to make any comments or suggestions to me, I would be very happy to receive them. Please call or write me.

I can't promise you that you'll get any responses, but what would happen if you followed up your note and letter to the editor with a phone call? Do you think that prospect/client would fail to talk to you?

Do you think any other stager or re-designer in your area would have reached out to that prospect in such a manner. Heck no!

What do you think would happen if you decided to become an advocate for the elderly or widows? If you saw some kind of injustice in your community, like recently aired on the Dr. Phil show (where victims of Hurricane Katrina were being victimized by unscrupulous contractors), and you wrote a Letter to the Editor exposing such activity and warning people of the injustice? I'm betting your letter would get printed.

Then if you turned around and started mailing a copy of your letter to every senior citizen or widow you know, or sending it to members of seniors clubs, do you think it would have a positive impact? Do you think that you might get some replies and that there might be an instant trust bond between you and those you connect with at that point? Of course there would be a closer bond.

I've said it before and I'll say it again, in the consulting business (no matter what industry you are in), people have to like you first. After they determine they like you, they must reach a point of trusting you. So after they like you and trust you, then they must see a benefit to whatever product or service you are presenting. If they can clearly see a benefit and they can afford it, they will hire you.

So by approaching them in a manner that shows them immediately that you are a good person and trying to do your part to look out for them, do you think the first hurdle of liking you and trusting you will be easier to achieve? You bet it will.

So start with your local newspaper. Look for clubs, industry publications, or newsletters that your target market subscribes to and see if you can champion some causes that are important to your niche market. It will go a long way to helping you build a strong client base within which you can become the "go-to" person, surpassing all your competitors.

By the way, if you have a professional folder of your services and/or a website, be sure and post copies of your Letters to the Editor or any other articles you've written there for people to read, or at least take note of. I practice what I preach. My main website, www.decorate-redecorate.com, is full of articles and tips that warn consumers of less than honorable tactics by people in my own industry, and a few outside my industry. I'm not just a trainer. I hope you'll think of me as an advocate for the home staging and re-design industry. Because of my training programs, many, many high priced seminar trainers have been forced to improve their programs and some have even lowered their fees. This has been good for you and others like you.

As a result, I don't seek out prospects any more. They come to me. I'm often treated like "royalty" by trainees and clients when they learn they are talking unawares to me on the phone. I'm not a celebrity. I'm not a guru. But I do have a wealth of insider knowledge and expertise that no one else has after 40 years in the design field – and I've proven myself as an advocate for the untrained, but talented, design entrepreneur.

12 Rules of Successful Networking

Every home stager and re-designer in the country should pay close attention to this section. Networking is an essential marketing tactic and strategy which you need to develop and master. So here are some brief guidelines that should govern your business practices.

Guideline #1 – _Develop a specific list of individuals who already have mastered the art of networking and are already influencing their own network. The people in their network must be the type of people that you want as your clients._

It's important to spend your quality time developing relationships with centers of influence. But the key is to dig deeper until you find the people who have a network of other people that they influence who are in the kind of target market you have pre-selected for your business.

So how do you figure that out, you ask? Well, you need to look closely at the area where you live and choose to work. Do some research and determine what industry groups in your area include the most wealthy individuals or families. This will be easier for some than for others.

Then you want to build relationships with influencers who have clients, or vendors or suppliers in that industry. Here's how you do that.

Let's say you have decided to specialize in the target market of physicians. You've learned that the majority of wealthy people in your area are in the medical field. Now you want to find out an influencer, who has a network of clients who are physicians.

Start with your own physicians and medical providers and ask them for the names and contact information of their accountants, attorneys, suppliers and service providers. You're not likely to get this information unless you've established a patient/doctor relationship already, but you never know unless you ask. Once you have put together a good sized list, you now turn around and check out each of these service providers.

Let's say you decide to start with all of the CPA's that are on the list. You want to interview each one of them, reviewing their credentials, evaluating their services and rating them for quality. You want to make sure than any CPA you choose to be involved with has a network of people he/she has influence over. That is vitally important.

You may get lucky and find someone who has a core of clients, vendors, suppliers who are not only in the medical profession, but who has plenty of clients who are attorneys as well. Bingo.

Your goal, then, is to pull together your own quality list – a custom network of your own – made up of the top influencers of physicians, surgeons and other medical personnel.

You know the saying, "It pays to shop around." I would bet that the best service providers, whether they are attorneys or CPAs, not only are influencers of an upscale network, they are highly skilled specialists in their own right. This should make it easy for you to recommend them to the cream of the crop in your area, whether they are in the medical profession or not.

By having your own custom network, you are bound to, over time, gain a valuable reputation as someone who can solve problems and make important connections for other people. And this, in turn, will provide you with wealthy clients who will be happy to connect you with other wealthy prospects.

Guideline #2 – _Don't align yourself with anyone who is not willing to include you as part of their influence network._

There are many people in life who are self-absorbed. They are what you would call "soviet-style" business people. These people are not interested in helping other people. Their sole interest is in helping themselves.

These are not the kind of influencers you want to connect with. To work out successfully over time, it has to be a win/win relationship.

Virtually everyone you might give a referral to will gladly accept it. But that doesn't mean that they will gladly add you to their network and pass referrals back to you. So this has to be established early on.

So I recommend a straight forward approach. Ask them if they will add you to their network on a conditional or probationary basis – say a trial period. You are wasting you valuable time if you become a client of theirs and they are not interested in adding you to their network.

So be smart. Determine in advance if they are open or not. You do this by asking for references. Then you call their clients to see if they have received network-related benefits or not. If not, move on.

Guideline #3 – _Look immediately for ways in which you can contribute to the wellbeing of the network. Offer your help._

I once belonged to a networking group. We gathered once a week at a hotel for breakfast and shared referrals. I was young and naïve. Every week I worked hard to come up with a few referrals to pass on and thought my fellow members would do the same. They did not.

The referrals I did get were weak and worthless. So this drives the point home all the more. The quality of the networks you gain admittance to must be one that is truly professional and members need to be focused on helping one another.

So what do you do if you are just starting out and you don't have any clients yet to share? Does this mean that you're out of the loop?

No. What you do is have a heart-to-heart talk with a highly successful professional with a network. You admit to this person that you are just starting out. You assure this person that you are hardworking, bright and honest – you simply don't have any clients as yet.

But then you go on and state that because of your hard work, your intelligence and your integrity, you will develop a strong client base over the course of your career.

 Tell the successful influencer that you recognize that they probably have many rookies among their network – other people who are new in their fields. Ask them to allow you to service those other rookies with the products and services that you offer. Tell this successful influencer that you will work very hard for these individuals, that you will serve them diligently and that you will honor whatever business they give you, even though you know it won't be very much.

I don't care who the influencer is, they are bound to remember how it was for them when they first started out and will probably admire you for your courage, determination and zeal.

So don't be afraid to approach them. Don't be anxious about approaching someone who is older and more successful than you. I mean, that's the whole point, isn't it? If you do this, you have everything to gain and nothing to lose. In time you will gain valuable endorsements and plenty of goodwill too.

Now let's take a slightly different route.

Schedule several dozen appointments with affluent business owners in your area. Your only mission is research.
Then set up appointments with selected CPAs, attorneys, service providers, suppliers and the like. With this group you say something like,

> *I'd like to show you a list of the affluent business owners with whom I've already had appointments and my appointment calendar for next month. I plan to visit several dozen of these types of prospects each and every month. I would love some of your business cards and would be happy to endorse you and your firm to them.*

Will their eyes light up? Wouldn't yours?

Naturally you won't want to approach anyone with a statement like this unless you are totally convinced they are a quality professional and worthy of your recommendations.

Guideline #4 – _See this as a long term commitment and understand that the benefits from your involvement will take time to develop. Be patient._

Now remember, don't see this as too much work on your part and too much time involvement. No business is built overnight. This process may take some time to bring about fruit, but it will be well worth it down the road.

If you focus on the short term, you won't want to do this method. It will be too slow. You will become impatient. And that would be a mistake on your part.

It takes years to develop your own influential network and it takes years to become an important part of other networks. Expect it to take 6 months to a year or longer to see any results. But if you hang in there and if you are tenacious, always keeping a smile on your face, the people you mingle with and network with will gain respect for you, and will enjoy you.

So give it time. Give it your all. You will succeed while others fail.

Guideline #5 – _Seek out the key influencers and devote more time and energy to building a relationship with them than with any of your peers, competitors, friends or colleagues._

Years ago I started an art business. I was introduced to the business through a multi-level art company out of Georgia called Transart Industries. They are no longer in business. The opportunity had two facets: sell their products (mainly through party plans and selling art to businesses) and by recruiting, training and directing. I was not at all interested in the party plan, but I was interested in building a business as a corporate art consultant and becoming a Director.

It would take 6 months of hard work to achieve the qualifications necessary to attend Director's School in Atlanta and then another 3 months of qualifying to actually become a Director.

I admired my trainer, so every time we were together in a group, I sought out her company. When we went somewhere as a group, I always tried to sit next to her and learn from her. No one told me to do that, but if you want to achieve the level of that person, and even surpass them, then you smartly attach yourself to them whenever possible.

I was one of a very tiny minority nationwide who achieved the rank of Director in the first 9 months of being in the business.

So I quite naturally expected my trainees to feel the same way and looked for them to try to attach themselves to me the way I had done. It didn't happen. Rather than trying to learn from the leader in their group, they seem to want to hang out with a member of my group who was charming and fun instead. But this gal achieved nothing. So they achieved nothing.

How foolish! If you attach yourself to a loser, you will more than likely be a loser yourself. This is why it is so important to guard yourself from people and influences that are negative. They will bring you down – guaranteed.

Move beyond those in your own industry. That means you must move beyond me. There's nothing wrong with keeping abreast of the home staging and redesign industry, but to be truly successful, you need to branch out.
Online "communities" where trainees can interact with each other can be helpful but they can also eat up valuable time better spent elsewhere. We plan to offer such a forum (check the website to see if it is launched), but caution you not to become dependent on it. Use it wisely to help you grow your business; just don't become addicted like some.

Many stagers and re-designers fail to become great because they focus on the wrong things (often taking advice from other beginners or negative thinkers). You've got to stay focused on "doing" the business.

Attorneys and CPAs are great sources for highly prized referral prospects. Are you focusing on the important players in the accounting and law professions? Focus on people like this. They have the ability to generate business for you by making one simple phone call! Get out of those "online communities", decorating discussion boards and membership sites. Build a business! Isn't that why you started?

Guideline #6 – _Look for ways to gain business for other people within the network, not for yourself._

I think it's interesting that it's often easier to sell the services and products of other people than to sell your own. I think that stems from the fact that we don't want to appear self-serving, boastful or pushy.

As you meet people, casually mention some of the names of professionals who are in your network. They could be accountants, attorneys, bank managers, loan officers, furniture rental managers and so forth.

And whenever you make a referral, follow it up with something in writing to both parties. This reinforces the fact to both parties that you have done them a favor by connecting them with each other.

Each side will feel a sense of gratitude and indebtedness to you. They will respect you and probably want to reciprocate in some way as soon as possible. They will also want to protect their reputation and be worthy of more referrals and connections from you in the future.

There is a saying in life that "what goes round, comes round". I'm sure you've heard of that before. There is another saying, "What comes out of your mouth, comes into your life." So by saying kind things and doing acts of kindness for others, you increase your chances of kind and good rewards coming your way. And you'll also feel very good about yourself too, because it feels good to give.

Guideline #7 – _Become a talent scout, publicist, advocate, data collector for the benefit of other members of the network._

At least once a month, select a few members of your network. Send them a note. Cut out articles you run across during the month and place them in a folder. These articles and tidbits that you find should be in the industry of the person you select. This will help them.

Look for people who are coming into a significant amount of money. Let them see that you understand the buying habits of affluent individuals, especially right after they receive a large amount of money. You could also write to your local newspaper or trade journal praising the work of individuals in your network. Then turn around and send the person a copy of the letter you wrote on their behalf.

You just might be successful in scoring an article for them in a paper or journal that they have failed to get into on their own. It is an easy and effective way to be remembered favorably by them in the future. Everyone likes to be recognized for their success and achievements. Most people are hesitant to toot their own horns.

You may even find, one day, that someone has written a glowing article about you and sent it in to the newspaper or trade journal in your industry. Wouldn't that be nice? If you know anything about publicity at all, you already know that 3rd party endorsements are far more valuable than your own statements about yourself.

But I bet you've never thought about sending in an endorsement for someone else to the media, much less that it could all be part of a larger strategy to build a profitable network for future business.

Guideline #8 – _Invite members of the network out for lunch, dinner, to a party or just for coffee. Entertain them._

You might live the lifestyle already of an affluent member of society. If you do, then you probably won't hesitate to invite clients or members of your network over to your home for dinner or to a party.

If you don't currently live in an upscale home, then you probably won't feel that comfort level. Not to worry. You can always host a dinner or party somewhere else: a fine restaurant, a park, the beach, a quality inn or hotel, someone else's home. Where there's a will, there's a way.
Did you know that the most successful marketers regularly entertain members of their network? Even if you're not playing host, you can join into recreational activities with them.

Networking should be fun. Don't spend all of your quality time associating with people in your own industry, family or relatives. Get beyond that.

Go to dinner with the affluent. Play golf with them or invite them to an art gallery or a craft fair. Have lunch with them in a business setting. Work with them as a volunteer. Get to know them on a personal basis, not just a business basis. This is one of the best ways to gain their trust. You gain their trust when you gain them as a friend.

Force yourself to socialize outside your comfort zone. You've got to hob knob with affluent people who have a network of their own before your networking efforts will start to pay off for you.

Guideline #9 – _**Intermingle and build relationships with more than one influential member. Try to find several.**_

It's important that you don't limit your relationships to just one attorney, or one CPA or one real estate agent. You don't have to do business with all of these people. But what you do have to do effectively is to let them know that you have the ability to enhance their reputation, their income, their business by connecting them with new clients.

Participate in their trade meetings and conferences. Do favors for them. Find speakers for their meetings and conferences. Do whatever it takes to help them grow and manage their businesses. It will eventually pay great dividends for your business.

Guideline #10 – _**Be very careful about who you endorse or recommend for products and services. Check them out first.**_

Protect your reputation. Select and recommend only those professionals with whom you are personally impressed. Do not refer anyone who is not qualified. You cannot afford to lose your credibility with members of your network.
I've put a new roof put on a home, replaced a balcony, had a home exterior repainted and fumigated, replaced a shower, upgraded parts of a kitchen, replaced windows and had a plumber repair some leaks.

I hired 8 sub contractors I had never hired before as I like periodically to try out new talent. However, I would recommend only one sub to other clients. That's how poor the servicing record was of the other 7 – and those were the best seven I interviewed for this project.

When you find that rare quality sub, hang on to them. They are worth gold to you.

I have built a network of subs for my business over the years. Some of my vendors are great and I expect to make them a lot of money for many years to come and profit nicely myself. I have fired some too. I cannot tolerate poor quality, poor communication and tardiness. You shouldn't either.

Guideline #11 – _Look for causes to get behind. Share your knowledge. Help others achieve their goals._

Consider volunteering your time for a charity. Many of the top affluent professionals and entrepreneurs are involved with causes. You could take this knowledge you are gaining and use it to help your favorite charity with fund-raising activities or to attract more volunteers.

Give away some of your expertise. You will look your best to prospects and clients when you give away your talent and expertise. Just look at the hundreds of free decorating tips pages I host on my website.

You'd be amazed at how many consultants never donate any time or help to charities. Did you know that the highest concentration of affluent prospects can often be found in charitable organizations helping the unfortunate? Need I say more?

Guideline #12 – _Become a recruiter for your network or organization. Bring in as many new members as you can._

Be on the lookout for new members to add to your network. Try not to look on sales people with disdain or as an irritant. They might just be perfect for your network and can keep you abreast of current information about new ways to make income and new market opportunities.

Interview them. Talk to attorneys, brokers, real estate agents, stockbrokers, financial consultants, accountants. Listen to the news. Watch TV shows featuring professionals from a wide background and variety of industries. You'd be amazed at the number of insider tips and facts that you can pick up and pass along to the right people at the right time.

This may sound funny, but I once had a multi million dollar top executive as an art client. He was turning 40 at the time and we got on the subject of hair loss. A few weeks before this meeting, I had heard an interesting fact about hair loss.

Noticing that he seemed to be worried about losing his hair, I mentioned to him that I had recently heard that a man will have virtually lost all of the hair he's going to lose by the time he is 40. You should have seen the relieved look that came over his face. He had a full head of hair at the time. I thought he was going to grab me and give me a huge hug.

A little thing to me, it made his day! Now, over 10 years later, he still has a full head of hair and I probably saved him from stressing out about that subject as he got older. I still remember that moment to this day. So you never know when something you might know will bless another person in a meaningful way, even though it has no impact on you personally.

While I didn't say anything at that moment to make him more money, I put him at peace on a subject that worried him. And I felt his gratitude though he never said anything more about the subject.

It's good to help other people.

Chapter 5
When to Contact the Affluent

Timing is such a critical factor to close the most deals, so you need to make sure you're not wasting your time. So in this chapter I'm going to give you some specific guidance to help you determine timing and minimize chasing after unproductive prospects.

Qualify Them First

Depending on the target market or niche market you have opted to focus upon, as you begin to collect prospects, it is vitally important that you qualify them. Not all affluent prospects will be worth the effort to pursue. Now it may be that falling into your niche is all the qualifying you need to do. Perhaps some of your prospects have serious money to spend. Regardless, you must spend your most valuable time on the prospects that prove to be your greatest opportunity.

Any prospect that already has a home on the market that hasn't sold right away is bound to be dissatisfied, either with themselves or their agent. Dissatisfaction is the "breeding ground" of opportunity for you.

Any prospect that does a lot of entertaining, who isn't completely proud of the way their home looks, is in a state of dissatisfaction. Think about your own home and situation. Are you totally satisfied with the way your home looks and functions? Chances are good that you are not.

A home on the market could also have already received staging services by a competitor. But guess what? Not all people who claim to be stagers know the first thing about proper staging techniques. Perhaps a home was managed by the realtor, who really hasn't studied staging techniques. Chances are very good that the homeowner is very unhappy. That means an opportunity for you. The owner already knows about the concept of staging, but the world is filled with so-called "professionals" who have done a miserable job.

While there is typically huge money to be made when there is a significant transfer of wealth, say from a business sale, the cashing in of stock options, switching a business from private to public, retirement, receiving an inheritance and so forth, there is also money to be made when a homeowner decides they have had enough. No one wants to live in an unsatisfied state for very long.

You've heard the saying, "Strike while the iron is hot". Well, the same is true for the sales professional or consultant. This is where timing becomes so crucial. Striking too early won't work. Striking too late is a disaster.

So be on the constant lookout for wealthy prospects who are in transition: they are or have recently come into a large sum of money or they are dissatisfied with products or services they have received to date.

If you read their industry publications, the newspaper and other articles, you'll glean lots of clues about key players. If you just listen to what people say around you, you'll also pick up on important clues. These will all help you hone in on your best prospects and opportunities and decide when it is best to contact them.

Listen for such things as: 1) an improvement they want to make right now; 2) a problem they want solved right now or soon; 3) an uncomfortable situation they are in and need to resolve; 4) a condition that worries them or frustrates them.

What Drives Their Purchase Decisions

More Americans have become affluent now than ever before in history. That's in large part due to the fact that baby boomers are on the far side of their careers. Earlier I said that most wealthy prospects are over 50 years of age and have families where the children have either left home or are about to do so.

This means that there are more major purchase decisions being made all around you. The wealthy are hard working, dedicated and very busy people. They are focused, quite often, on three things: 1) running a business; 2) climbing the corporate ladder; 3) maintaining what they have built.

They never have enough time in a day to accomplish what they set out to accomplish. They expect your full time attention and they won't tolerate hassles.

Add to that these common factors:

- They demand respect. After all they have achieved much and might even want to be honored for it.
- They have become successful, in part, because of their own professional standards and competence. So quite naturally they expect that same level of professionalism from everyone else.
- They have strong feelings about deception or manipulation. If they feel deceived, they will immediately take their business elsewhere. Being late for an appointment with them can have drastic implications. They don't like someone making them wait and wasting their time.
- They don't mind researching before making a decision and they will trust their own judgment. The internet has given them a very easy way to research. Give them the facts and they will arrive at the best decision with little or no advice from anyone else.
- They will determine the value of a product or service according to their own standards and terms, which are probably going to be quite different from the norm.
- Once they find the value they seek, they have no qualms about shopping online or even at a discount warehouse. They like a bargain just as much as anyone else.
- They are not interested in "keeping up with the Joneses". They want to "be different from the Joneses" or "ahead of the Joneses". And they can afford to be different and a front runner.
- Hassles are not something they will tolerate. They have enough hassles to contend with in their careers. They will expect great service and things to be done when promised and as promised.
- They can afford to hire the best. They want the best information they can get, the best products they can get, the best competence and expertise money will buy, and the best service available. If you're not prepared to give them that, go away.

The Transfer of Wealth

So let's discuss once again the all important timing issues relating to the transfer of wealth, because this is such a critical part of the process for you. Transfer of wealth is only significant when it involves an extra large amount all at one time – something happening that is out of the ordinary in your prospect's life. It is important to you because right after a transfer of a large amount of money, your prospect will be extremely happy and wanting to spend some or all of the money.

- There is the sale of a business
- They have signed a big contract
- There is the sale of stock
- There is a profit when a company goes public
- Perhaps a large bond has matured
- There is dissatisfaction with a current realtor, stager or designer
- They are preparing to retire and downsize
- They have discovered a lucrative real estate deal
- They have received an inheritance
- A divorce has taken place
- They are just wanting to renovate or update or add on
- Adult kids have moved back home unexpectedly

By knowing in advance or at the time that a transfer of wealth is about to take place or has just taken place, you will have your greatest opportunities to differentiate yourself from the competition. You will not merely be listing your services like everyone else, you'll be able to demonstrate a deeper value. And value is what the affluent look for.

Building Lasting Relationships

Your commitment to building lasting relationships with affluent prospects is vitally important if you ever want to reach the pinnacle of success as a stager or re-designer. I'm not talking about short term relationships. I'm talking about long term friendships. And you must be proactive, not reactive. Always keep the initiative on your side. Stay committed.

Begin by making sure that everyone connected with your business is on the same page as you are. That means your spouse, children, partners and employees. Everyone must understand the commitment to excellence and the importance of building relationships.

As in any friendship or relationship, both parties seek something from the relationship to benefit themselves. Your prospect or client may be looking for solutions; you are looking to provide solutions. In the process of getting to that point, you would do well to seek to provide them with information, ideas, tips and helpful tidbits that go beyond the obvious. In the aftermath of doing business, you would do well to maintain the relationship, continuing to pass on help to your client that goes beyond the project itself.

By continuing the relationship after the business portion has concluded, you will reinforce your commitment to a friendship or mentoring role. Your client will continue to look to you for advice and help and from time to time will probably be happy to send new business your way, either from referrals they give you or additional projects they hire you for themselves.

Recently I invited a niche market landscaper to come to my home and design a plan to renovate my back yard. I had done a lot of research over the internet for specific items that I thought would look nice and fit the overall theme I wanted.

The landscaper and I discussed what I wanted and what I didn't want,

 he took full measurements and I showed him all of the pictures of products that I wanted incorporated into the design.

He left saying he would put together a proposal. About a week later I got an email proposal which roughly itemized various portions of the project. The grand total was for $50,000.

There was no sketch or design of any kind included with the proposal. I am a visual person and while I appreciated the facts and figures, I needed to see a rough layout (at the very minimum) of what I would be getting for my $50,000. So I requested a layout.

A couple days later I got one by email.

I haven't responded, and now it is about 3 months later and I have never heard from the landscaper again.

Now he either has more work than he can handle, or he has totally failed to learn the most basic concepts of building a relationship with a prospect. Perhaps my project was small in comparison to commercial projects that he handles.

I don't know, but $50,000 seemed like a tidy sum for just a back yard.

What I'm saying is that this landscaper has invested absolutely no effort to find out why I didn't respond. He has not put forth any effort at all to get to know me, to share anything helpful with me, to bond with me in any way, much less ask for my business.

As a result, he will not be hired.

You've got to ask for the business in some way. You've got to show that you want the business. If you abandon your prospect along the way, if you don't build a relationship with an affluent prospect, you won't get nearly the business you could get, and you may not get any business at all.

Making Seamless Presentations

The more affluent the prospect, the greater is the need for your sales process to become seamless – by that I mean hardly or barely noticeable. Closing the sale cannot be forced. It needs to come out of the natural process of giving your client advice and help. It must be a logical conclusion of what has gone before.

Therefore, you need to rid yourself of any kind of "sales pitch" when dealing with wealthy prospects. You do this by replacing a sales presentation with the art of asking questions. By asking questions, you will be able to discover important information about your prospects, their families, their business or career. Then you will know if you have a service or product that will meet their needs and desires.

People buy because they need something or want something. If they can't see your service or product benefiting them in any way, they won't buy anything or hire you to do anything for them.

You must get rid of anything in your seamless process that might suggest in any way that you are being deceptive or manipulative. If they see that in you, the relationship will terminate immediately.

In the landscape illustration above, I felt that the proposal was a bit deceptive. With no visual presentation to support the facts and figures, I was at a total loss as to what would be included in my landscape design.

I can't imagine being in a visual business and not giving my prospect some kind of visual example of what my design included. It blew me away. Did this landscaper actually expect me to plunk down $50,000 on the basis of a two page itemization? Did he expect me to accept his proposal on blind faith that he would translate his proposal into a design that met my expectations? What was he thinking?

I have no idea.
For a $50,000 project, he should have put together a nice visual presentation, hand delivered to my home. He should have made an appointment and sat down with me to show me his plan and explain the figures and inquire as to whether I felt the design included what I wanted or needed to be tweaked. Had he done that, he probably would have been hired.

He came across as a disinterested salesman. He came across as being a bit deceptive and cutting corners. I'm very opinionated. I know what I want. I'm a strong decision maker. And since I'm in sales myself, I'm very aware of sales techniques. I don't like pushy salespeople. I don't like people who waste my time. And I don't trust people who don't do a good job in helping me thoroughly understand their product or service.

I also don't care for sales people who don't have an opinion that they are willing to stand behind. A kitchen remodeling saleslady once came to my home to give me an estimate on remodeling my kitchen. She showed me samples of the products her company offered for counters. Every time she saw me look at a specific sample and show some interest, that particular sample became the best she had to offer. If after telling me that one color was best I drifted away and showed interest in another color, then she switched her opinion, and now the new sample became the best she had to offer.

After switching her sales pitch 5 or 6 times, I grew weary of her and dismissed her company as a prospective subcontractor. I'm not interested in someone whose advice changes with every breeze. Form an opinion as to what you believe to be the best course your client can take and stick with it, and also support it by pointing out the benefits which elevate it above the other options. They will see right though you and distrust you if your advice bends and sways all the time.

Keep everything you do framed in the context of "consultation" services. You are there to assist them. Rapport is necessary. Some sales organizations refer to this process as "profiling". I prefer to call it "conceptual selling". By presenting a total concept that meets the needs of your prospect, they won't feel like you are "selling" them, nor will you.

If you don't ask questions, you won't know how to fit your product or service to their needs. When you go on a fact finding mission, you can then easily related the information as to how the inner workings of your business will meet their needs. Part of the process includes giving them competitive alternatives to select from, and then discussing price points and their options, warranties, terms and conditions.

Done right, your prospect will be able to make an intelligent decision that is right for him or her. They won't feel hassled or pushed, they won't feel stressed or "sold" and they will respect you and trust you. And therein is the secret to building a huge, successful consultation business.

Offering Convenience

The rich expect to get a certain amount of pampering. They feel they deserve it. Some might even feel insulted if they are not given priority status.

I've noticed something interesting on the highway. In former years when my income was dramatically lower than it is today, I drove older cars.

I noticed that in an older car, other drivers tended to not yield to me when I clearly had the right of way. If there was a doubt as to who had the right of way, they clearly paid me no respect and took the right of way.

Now that I drive a nicer vehicle, I get more respect on the road. I don't find other drivers trying to cut me off and when I have earned the right of way, I am usually allowed to proceed first.

So what's the difference? The difference is the perceived value that people give to me now in a newer vehicle than I received in an older, worn car. It's a matter of respect. It's a matter of value.

While it isn't right or fair, the fact of the matter is that the more affluent you get, the more respect you tend to get. Whether you deserve more respect or not doesn't seem to matter. You get it just by virtue of appearing more successful than the average person.

So it stands to reason, that if the general public automatically tends to treat wealthy people with more respect and grant them more favor out in public or in the work place, it naturally follows that those who are wealthy expect special treatment from others all the time.

And because they have come to expect special attention and a higher priority level of treatment, you'd better be willing and able to deliver it or you won't go very far building a business that caters to luxury clients. This is why I pointed out the failure of the landscaper to impress me. Not only did he not treat me with any kind of special service, he didn't even give me basic, ordinary service.

Like it or not, when serving the wealthy, you need to have a servant's attitude. When they say "Jump", you need to respond quickly with "How high?" You need to be willing to go the extra mile for them. And you need to do it with a smile, because if you show any resentment or reservation, they will pick up on it.

So when you're setting appointments with the affluent prospect, you need to make yourself available to them **at their convenience**, not yours. If they need to see you after hours or on weekends, you need to be available when they can see you. You'll have to juggle your schedule, make special arrangements if necessary, and do whatever it takes to make doing business with you as easy and uncomplicated as possible.

If your prospect has to make exceptions or special time for you that is inconvenient for them, they likely will turn you down altogether. As much as you'd like all appointments to take place at a convenient time for you, it just isn't going to work out that way.

So if you have to travel to and fro in the midst of heavy work traffic, you do it. If you have to give up your weekend to meet a deadline, you do it. If you have to make extra trips to accommodate them, you do it. If you are making a presentation, you do it in person, not by fax or email. You go the extra mile. Of course, we should treat every prospective or current client like this whether they are wealthy or not, but it's especially critical to do so with the upscale market.

Whenever I discuss setting an appointment with a client, I always ask them, "What is your schedule like? When is the most convenient time for you to meet with me? Would a weekday work best for you or do you need a weekend?"

Whatever they tell me, I jump through hoops to accommodate them.

My son has a DJ business and he operates with a cell phone. The first time I called his phone, he didn't answer, so I got his message. He informed me that he couldn't take the call at the moment, and asked me to leave my phone number and name.

But then he went on to say, "I'll call you back at my earliest convenience." Whoa. Not good. He should have said, "I'll call you back as soon as possible." So be careful how you phrase things to people. You never want them to think that they have to accommodate you – you're supposed to be making life convenient and easy for them, not the other way around.

Offering Quality Products

I cannot stress enough the importance of offering quality products and services that are full of value. Everything you say and do must be upscale. All of your terms must be upscale. All of your options must be upscale.

And you should strive to find a way to enable your wealthy clients to utilize your products and services in a manner that is uniquely theirs. Remember what I said about them wanting to be "different from the Joneses".

You must also make everything perfectly clear, perfectly understood. These people have already done their homework, whether you know they have or not. They may even present themselves as being naïve, all the while sizing you up from a position of being thoroughly informed on the subject.

I met recently with a major corporation to discuss the design needs for a building they had upgraded. They needed special help with personalizing and branding the building with their corporate logo and image. At one point in the discussion, I specifically asked the facility manager if they had a budget. She told me "no". That was a lie. Because we had inside information, we knew that she had already been given a budget and we even knew the numbers. But she did not know we knew.

You should know that what your prospect tells you might not be true - especially when establishing a budget. I understood where she was coming from and the "game" she was playing, but what she didn't know was that I was sizing her up to determine if I even wanted to handle the project. In the end, I told her that we were not a good fit and wished her well in finding another company to assist her. I walked away from a $40,000 project because I couldn't trust her.

We also had difficulty communicating with one another and she did not have the authority to make the final decisions regarding the project. The real decision maker is the person you want to work with whenever possible.

My time is extremely valuable too. I prefer not to waste it trying to work with non-decision makers. You always need to qualify your prospects and agree to meet only with the individual(s) who have the power to hire you. If the husband makes the decisions, find that out. Meet with him. If the wife makes the decisions, find that out. Meet with her instead. As previously mentioned, wives are more often than not the decision makers regarding home décor. Don't assume that she must consult with her husband first.

I have been insulted many times when a salesman assumed that he had to meet with both me AND my husband. I make decisions all the time without any input from my husband. To assume that I am incapable of making a major buying decision under my own power is a misconception that many males hold. And it has been a major mistake on their part, because if I feel insulted, you can bet I won't do business with that salesman.

Some businesses have made an initial impact in their industry. Here in the USA, people love new products and services. But if your products and services do not have great value, your business will not be able to sustain itself. In my own business, I have worked diligently for over 6 years to build my training programs. They have improved every year and I'm proud of that fact. While the format and presentation were not always the best, the content has been very well received by almost everyone who has done business with me.

And as time goes by, I hope to reach a point where my products and services will make 100% of my clients feel happy and satisfied. And you should make the same kind of commitment with regard to what you offer. There is no substitute for quality and value.

I might not win over everyone, but I do know one thing, and that is that there is no other home staging and redesign trainer in the world that offers the value that I offer.

As a result, one of my vendors just wrote me this week and told me that she has noticed that I am the only client she has who never seems to have a slow down.

Periodically you need to re-evaluate everything you are doing to see if there are ways you can improve. I will always be working to make my business reach for a higher and higher standard of quality. You should too.

Offering Quality Service

When one thinks of quality service, it comes as no surprise that you might think of the Ritz-Carlton Hotel chain. That's because the Ritz-Carlton believes that service **after** the sale is just as important as service is **before** the sale. As our economy becomes more and more driven to the internet and communicating via email, voice mail, pagers and fax machines, we are forcing our clients to service themselves more than ever before.

Are you surprised that an internet marketer and trainer like me would point out the dangers of becoming overly virtual? Well, even though I have structured my business to serve my clients virtually, I'm not at all forgetful of the importance of keeping some measure of personal service in the works.

This is why, if you call my office, you'll often find that I answer the phone myself. I have a small staff, but I want my clients to know that I'm relatively easy to reach (at least for now). I have to function at a virtual level due to the huge popularity of my training programs and products, but I also recognize that the personal touch is highly prized, especially by the affluent individual.

But your business is not like mine. You are a consultant working out in the home environment. It is mandatory that you be as personable as possible. It is mandatory that you be reachable by phone and in person. It is ideal to handle all of your business, or as much as possible, in person – face to face.

Remember, the goal is not just to make the first sale. The goal is far more long term than that. The goal is to build a relationship with every affluent client that is long lasting. Not just for the referrals, but it's a whole lot easier to sell more products and services to people who have purchased or dealt with you in the past than it is to develop a new client.

I must admit that I'm not 100% perfect in my servicing of clients. But I try hard. Much of my business is automated, and sometimes the automation breaks down through no fault of my own. But thankfully that is rare. Still that's not much consolation to a frustrated client whose expectations, according to my claims or their own ideas, were not met. I cannot, of course, be responsible for assumptions visitors make to my website. People sometimes don't read all of the copy or they interpret it to mean something it is not actually saying. That will always happen to some degree, but whenever it happens, I try to revisit the website to see if there can be a way to avoid further complaints, whether they were spawned by me or not.

No matter how you structure your business, you will encounter problems from time to time. At least I hope your problems will be rare. Mine are. But whenever you deal with people, their expectations and personalities and goals, you'll have problems of one sort or another. How you handle them is important.

Ideally you want to handle the situation in a manner that makes the client happy and that solves whatever problem arose. That is not always possible, however. There are times when a client will request something that is unreasonable.

In my business, the unreasonable requests usually come in the form of wanting a special price, a special discount or some other consideration not offered to anyone else. And while I might wish I could accommodate the request, I do refuse to give something to one person that I don't give to everyone. And that goes for the wealthy trainee and the poor trainee. I feel that I would undermine my personal and corporate integrity if I did not hold fast to the rules and regulations, terms and conditions, deadlines and such that my website describes.

From time to time I have changed those terms and conditions, and I reserve the right to do that and to do it without advance warning or notification. That is my right. It is also my obligation to be fair to everyone, regardless of their circumstances or social standing.

So it won't do anyone any good to call me or write me asking for a payment plan and giving me a hardship story. While I privately might have a great deal of empathy for someone going through a hard time in their life, I've been there in my life too and I never asked for special consideration as a result.

But there are many people who have a sense of entitlement and think that the world owes them special favors. There are also people who try to con you, lie to you and twist the truth in an attempt to favor themselves. So be aware.

Having said that, you still need to strive for and achieve the happiness and satisfaction of every client. And you should never assume that an affluent client is happy. Some people have no qualms about complaining. They can even be rude and insulting. But there are others who are unhappy and never let on. They just cross you off the list for future business or referrals.

So in your attempt to please the upscale client, you have to assume that they are not happy and check in with them to see if you are mistaken. And if you discover there is a problem, you need to correct it immediately. The longer the problem exists, the greater frustration your client will experience and that is not good.

As soon as I find out that a client of mine is experiencing a problem, I drop everything I am doing and I work to resolve the issue. I don't think there is any other way to conduct business.

Remember that it is the post-service you give that will be the last thing about you and your business a client will experience. Don't give them any reasons to find that you didn't measure up.

Being Efficient

If you are not efficient you will immediately annoy your affluent client. Remember we've already discussed the fact that wealthy prospects are extremely busy. So don't waste their time.

Never be late for an appointment. It's insulting to them and you'll be starting off on the wrong foot. I have terminated vendors for being late to the first appointment. I figure that if they are late when they are most eager to impress me, what will happen later if I hire them and their motivation to impress me is gone?

Try not to make your wealthy clients fill out forms. At least keep it to a bare minimum. They don't like to fill out forms and consider it as an annoyance. If you have forms that need to be filled out, fill them out yourself. Then all you have to ask for is their signature.

Speed up the time it takes to get started. Cut the red tape for them. Keep your integrity, but do what you can to protect their time and energy. That is often why they select one company over another.

Think of yourself as a high priced problem solver. Never think of yourself as a salesperson. Make sure every prospect, every client, every vendor or supplier knows that you are their "go-to" trouble shooter. Work to make sure every detail is handled properly and in a timely manner.

And to make certain you are immediately alerted to any problem as soon as possible, it would be a good idea to give every affluent prospect and client your private cell phone number or pager number. Since I have a huge number of clients to service, I can best service them efficiently by email, and that is why my most valued clients and trainees get my personal email address.

Chapter 6
How to Contact the Affluent

Marketing Your Business

You are a consultant. Yes, you specialize in home staging and/or interior redesign, but at face value you are a consultant. At least that is the best way to market your business. The last thing you want people to think about you is that you're a home cleaner or a furniture mover. You never want to come across as someone who does manual labor. I'm not saying that there is anything wrong with manual labor, but you want to be viewed as a consultant, because consultant's can command (and get) higher fees for their expertise and services, but more importantly you are a consultant because you've been, or are being, trained to be one. This means you have knowledge the general public does not have, so they hire you for your knowledge. If they only need a "furniture mover", they could hire one for a lot less money.

How you market your business is the key to whether you will be successful or not. Success lies not in whether you are certified or not. It lies, not in how talented you are nor in how creative you are, but in how successfully you prove to prospects that what you offer has value for them.

Success will be determined by how successfully you market and promote your business and how you carry yourself. In the consulting fields, face to face dealings are critical to success. You see, you will be selling yourself in addition to the knowledge, products and services you offer.

Face-to-face communication is the best and richest form of communication you will ever get. And in an age where technology is taking over the whole realm of communication, face-to-face communication is quickly becoming a lost art.

Face-to-face communication is vitally important when you first meet someone as that is the time they are quickly determining if you are the type of person they can like and trust. And in face-to-face communication, only 7% of what you say will stick with the prospect. A whopping 93% of your communication will come from a combination of what you sound like (38%) and how you look (55%). This is what is referred to as "non-verbal" communication.

So it is clear that your non-verbal communication is much stronger than your verbal communication. To break it down further, your non-verbal communication includes the following aspects: 1) your body language; 2) your posture; 3) your facial expression; 4) your eye movements; 5) your wardrobe; 6) how you respond to the other person's comments and gestures; 7) the distance between you and the other party; 8) the short responses you make ("aha", "yes", "no", "ok", "I understand"); 9) your hand movements; 10) your attentiveness and focus on the other party.

Since much of what you will communicate will be messages that happen automatically, and since you have no control over how another person will react to you, here are a few tips to help you better your chances of being well received.

Getting Them to Know You

Smiling is the absolute first thing you should make sure you do when you first meet someone. Some people seem to walk around with a smile planted permanently on their face. Even the corners of their mouth turn upward, making it look like they are smiling even if they are not.

I'm not one of those people. I have come to find out that I don't smile readily, so I have to concentrate on smiling more. Hopefully you're not like me in that department.

Did you know that the average person can create over 10,000 different facial expressions? There are even different degrees of smiles, from a full laughing smile to the Mona Lisa-type partial smile.

A full, complete smile is the absolute best way to generate the beginning of your face-to-face communication and get it off to a pleasant start.

Because the first few minutes are so crucial, practice doing the following:

- Get plenty of rest each day. You never know when you will meet someone for the first time, and you want to be alert and cheerful for any exchange you have.
- Since we all shake hands with our right hand, try to carry your purse or other items in your left hand to make it easier to extend your hand quickly toward the other person to grasp it.

- Smile warmly and immediately. My tension is held in my mouth so I have to remember to relax my face and smile naturally. It might help to think of something pleasant just before you know you're going to meet someone new.
- Everyone likes to hear their name spoken by other people. So make sure you repeat the person's name, that you pronounce it correctly and that you say it with confidence.
- Don't extend a hand that is limp. Shake hands confidently, but don't squeeze the other person's hand. I have had men shake my hand so hard they have actually hurt me. I've even had a few women hurt me as well. I like a firm handshake. I totally hate a fish-like handshake and it always makes me think the other person is overly timid and lacks confidence.
- Know in advance how you want to introduce yourself. It should include your name and a very brief sentence that sums up who you are. Practice it in front of a mirror. Be sure to smile as you practice.
- Be ready at all times with ideas for small talk. Focus the small talk that you initiate on the other person.

Your Self Introduction

The type of self introduction you use should be tailored to the situation and the person you are meeting. You will have different goals in mind, so the introduction should fit the goal.

Promote Your Company
"Hello, I'm Mary Smith with MyCompanyName"

When Referred by a Client
"Hello, I'm Mary Smith. I'm the home staging specialist for Janet Jones and her family."

When Referred by a Mutual Friend
"Hi, I'm Mary Smith. We have a mutual friend, Janet Jones."

You Have a Personal Connection with the Person
"Hello, I'm Mary Smith, and I understand we attend the same church."

Always remember that at this point in time, _you_ are the product, not your company, not your service, not the products you sell.

In as comfortable manner as possible, you want to guide the conversation so that the other person eventually asks you, "What do you do for a living?" By telling the person how you are connected with someone else, you are subtly sending the message that you can do the same for them.

When the question comes, you say, "I handle the home staging (or redesign) affairs for a select group of families."

By adding the phrase "a select group of families" you will probably peek their interest, so you must be ready for follow-up questions.

Getting Them to Like You

It should be no secret to anyone that, in most cases, people love to talk about themselves. I will admit it. I am, in many ways, most interested in myself. Go on. Admit it. You are most interested in you. That is human nature.

Well, the affluent prospect/client is no different than you or me. So one of the best ways to get them to like you is to deliberately get them talking about themselves. This is of extreme benefit to you.

First, when you focus your attention on them, you will be more relaxed. It's much easier to ask questions than it is to answer questions. And since the focus of attention is on the other person, it will help you be yourself, even if you feel a bit uncomfortable.

At the same time you are becoming more comfortable and relaxed, the other person will probably start to feel at ease in your company. They are talking about their favorite subject – so they will be happy and will think you are a terrific person for being interested in them.

Steer clear of subjects like religion and politics. Those subjects can become volatile, heavy and sources of conflict. Avoid talking about the weather. That's boring. Make the time together count for something.

Keep in mind your short term and long term goals. Don't rush in about your business. It's important to demonstrate a genuine interest in the other person, what they do for a living, how they became successful, what they foresee in their immediate and long term future, even some tidbits about their family.

Don't be overwhelmed by the fact that the prospect is wealthy. No matter what one's net worth is, no one person is more valuable as a person than anyone else. Their time might be more valuable. Their bank account may have more digits. But as far as basic human value, we all are equal to each other.

You will find success easy to achieve in the face-to-face meeting if you show a strong interest in the other person and if you are good at getting the other person to talk about himself/herself. Believe me, if you have carried on a conversation with someone for 3-5 minutes, and you have devoted the majority of the time focused on the other person, you should then find it quite easy to steer the conversation in a way that motivates that person to ask you, "What do you do for a living?"

Getting Them to Trust You

Trust will be impossible to achieve if your prospect or client does not like you. So getting them to like you is the first hurdle. The next hurdle is getting them to trust you. By trusting you, I mean getting them to rely on your ability to deliver what you offer and getting them to believe that you have their best interests at heart.

And we're not just talking about trust in the moment. We're also talking about creating a way for your prospect to trust you long term – today, tomorrow, next week, next month, next year.

Yesterday a trainee prospect asked me, "What do I do to make sure that a homeowner doesn't come back to me later and want a refund if their house doesn't sell?" She's not even in the business yet and already she's worried that an owner will be unhappy with her work and want a refund.

With that kind of fear, she will have a tough time convincing others to trust her, because she is afraid to trust herself. Certainly one needs to draw up agreements that protect them and this type of thing should be addressed in the contract, but to be unduly afraid of it before you've even entered a business means you may be starting at a disadvantage right out of the blocks – a disadvantage you've placed on yourself and one that only you can remove.

Trust must begin with you. You must trust yourself. You must have confidence in your own abilities, your ability to communicate effectively and your ability to put procedures and policies in place that are professional and standard to any service of this kind.

If you don't believe in yourself, no one else will believe in you. This is the point where many would-be stagers and re-designers get cold feet and never even get their businesses off the ground. They just can't overcome their own personal fears and doubts. Fear is the great immobilizer.

So first realize that most of what you fear is just imagined. Recognize that what you fear will probably never happen. It's not only true for staging and redesigning, it's also true for life. Many people spend their whole lives fearful of this or that and some even become fanatical about it. And that's a real shame. There are just as many people afraid to succeed as there are people afraid to fail.

So trust starts with trusting yourself.

Once you fully trust yourself, then you are ready to set the stage for other people to trust you.

Start by getting rid of anything in your process that smacks of being a "salesman" or "saleswoman". One of the first things sales people do is to place a brochure or other piece of material in the prospect's hand. Resist the urge to do that. The last thing you want to do is come across as a salesperson.

Next, don't try to be overly friendly, overly knowledgeable, or overly anything. It makes you appear phony. It makes you appear to be someone trying too hard to sell and their defense mechanisms will just go up. Wouldn't yours? A good example of this affected phoniness is the telemarketer calling total strangers and asking them, "How are you today?" as if they really care how you are. My personal pet peeve is someone calling me up and not identifying themselves immediately or acting as if I know them personally when I don't.

Instead, be patient. Spend your time showing how interested you are in them. Ask questions. Be yourself. Laugh at their jokes – hopefully you'll have a few of your own. Let a friendship get planted first and begin to grow. Water the friendship. Nurture the relationship.

As you build a genuine relationship, you will start to display credibility and integrity. Both of these concepts are intertwined in the road to building trust. Be believable and trustworthy. That will give you credibility. Set for yourself some moral principles by which you conduct business. This will establish your integrity and keep you from veering away from it.

It may take a little time, but when your prospect sees evidence of your credibility and integrity over time, you will gain their trust. When you do this, you'll find that your whole process of getting to know them and bringing them to a point of hiring you will be seamless, effortless and very, very rewarding.

Here are some ways to check yourself to make sure you moving in the right direction:

- Did you arrive on time?
- Did you handle the critical first 4 minutes in a professional manner?
- Did you introduce yourself smoothly?
- Did you repeat their names and pronounce them correctly?
- Were you dressed appropriately?
- Did you speak distinctly and clearly?
- Did you make any negative comments or critical comments?
- Did you avoid talking about anything controversial?
- Did you allow them to do most of the talking?
- Did you encourage them to talk about their interests?
- Did you sincerely make them feel important and respect them?
- Did you look for their style and adapt yours to fit theirs?
- Did you focus on possible solutions and tactics and not on your products or services?
- Did you have a business card handy when asked for one?

Your success will be determined by how many of those questions you were able to answer with a "yes".

But we're not done yet. The above questions were just for the first meeting. Remember, you're trying to build a lasting relationship with this prospect or client. So now answer these questions after your next meetings:

- Did you continue to be on time for all appointments?
- Have you always returned phone calls promptly?
- Have you responded to every communication (phone call, email, fax message) you've received from the prospect within 24 hours?
- Did you ever make the mistake of saying "trust me"?
- Did you ever make up an answer to a question instead of just admitting you don't know but that you will research it and get back to them?
- Were you ever evasive in your answers?

- Did you ever fail to do something you promised you would do?
- Did you lie about anything?
- Did you mislead them in any way?
- Did you maintain eye contact with them at all times?

How well you did on these questions only you will know. But if you are guilty of any failure along the way, you bring into serious doubt your credibility and your integrity. These are the things that will hurt your business, I guarantee it.

A young woman was recently attending a social event and afterwards was in a networking opportunity. A very, very well known magician was there and she began to notice that he definitely noticed her. After a while, when she had her back to the magician, she felt a tap on her shoulder. Turning around, the magician said, "What's your ethnicity?"

Now this entertainer was quite attractive and she had always been fascinated by his work and was delighted to meet him. After a while, he asked her for her phone number and she gave it to him. He was from the East Coast and said he'd really like to get together with her before he returned to home.

The next morning he called her at 9:30 AM and asked her to call him back. She didn't get the message right away but did return his phone call in the early afternoon. He told her he couldn't talk right then as he was heading into a meeting but that he would call her back in about an hour.

He never called back.

Naturally the young lady was quite disappointed as she had looked forward to getting to know him. But it never materialized.

She had just learned a very important thing about this man's integrity and that it was a good thing to learn so quickly that he couldn't be trusted. She'll come to realize that the man lacks integrity and actually did her a favor by showing his true colors so quickly.

Unfortunately, life if full of people who do not do what they, of their own choice, volunteer to do. Not only did this man walk away from a truly genuine person who had previously admired him greatly, he lost a fan.

And word about his reputation will now go out to several of her friends and no doubt several of their friends, and so on and so on.

How easy it would have been to simply say, "Gee, I had a window of opportunity to see you earlier in the day and now I can't, I'm very sorry, but thank you for returning my call."

By being honest, he would have signaled a level of integrity and kept a fan or two or three or whatever, and they might have eventually developed a friendship that would have been a blessing to both of them. That will never happen now.

To summarize, let me give you a list of things your prospects/clients will need from you in order to trust you:

- Always place their interests ahead of your own.
- Always be on time – always – to everything – with everything
- Don't be overly serious – have some humor when possible
- Respond quickly – I mean quickly – certainly within 24 hours
- State what your next action will be and do it – don't ever say "trust me"
- Never make up answers but promise to find the answers – and then give them the correct answers
- Be specific and clear with everything you say and do
- Never lie to them or mislead them intentionally – you can't do much about things people assume, but try to minimize what they assume to be true that is not
- Always look them in the eye
- Always try to add even more meaning and value to the relationship as time goes by
- Never promise what you can't or won't deliver (remember the magician story)
- Over deliver on your promises

To illustrate further, a young woman just called me on the phone for information. She had been referred to my website and was looking for a way to work as a home stager for someone else, rather than starting her own business. My first objective when talking to her was to find out what her goals were. If I don't know a person's goals, how am I going to give them any sensible direction?

My next objective was to simply explain how we could help her achieve her goals and eventually I led her back to the website to get the full details of how I could help her get where she wanted to go. I asked her if she had been to the website and she said "no". She didn't know the name of it so I gave it to her. But when she wrote it down, she wrote down "un-decorate" instead of "re-decorate". I corrected the mistake with humor and we both laughed. She said, "I thought there was something wrong. Why would you decorate just to un-decorate?"

The conversation ended on an upswing due to the humor and my ability to help her laugh about the mistake and get it corrected. I have no doubt whatsoever that this lady will become a student, not because of what I said particularly, not maybe even because of what I offer, but because we made a connection and she trusts me.

I did not try to sell her anything but just suggested she look over the various options at her disposal and make a decision based on what's comfortable for her. Had she told me that she was definitely interested in building a career as a home stager, then I probably would have taken the time to give her more information over the phone about my career courses, but as it was I fit the conversation to her and the goals she gave me - a soft sell approach – even though she approached me.

You can never go wrong by trying your best to do what's right for the prospect or client.

Give Them Respect

I'm currently approaching senior citizen status. I've been around the block a time or two - or ten. I've had a few failures. I've had several successful businesses. I know a thing or two. I'm not perfect. Don't try to be. I am who I am. But thousands of people come to me for training. While I can't do anything about whether they take and use what they learn or not, I have upheld my end of the bargain.

I'm reminded of the movie "A Few Good Men" with Jack Nicolson, Demi Moore and Tom Cruise. At a pivotal point in the movie, respect becomes a clear issue as Tom Cruise (attorney) orders Jack Nicolson (witness) to sit back down in the witness chair. Jack exclaims to the Judge, "Tell him to address me as Colonel. I think I've **earned** it." The judge replies, "And you will address **me** as Judge. **I'm certain I've earned it.**"

Well, I'm certain I've earned it too.

Donald Trump admitted on his show (The Apprentice) that he doesn't take kindly to criticism and that he "never forgets it", implying that those that don't give him respect are forever remembered and blacklisted. I have to admit I'm much the same.

Have the common sense to know your place. Being uppity and self-indulgent isn't going to win you any awards, nor respect. And I guarantee you, you'll discover at some point that you have lost more than you hoped to gain.

I shudder at the thought that highly critical people enter our industry. I worry about the disrespect they will give out to their clientele. Invariably too, they always turn out to be people who cannot back up their claims. So if you just can't resist throwing out darts, make sure all your ducks are in a row first. It's easy to point out the speck in someone else's eye. But what about the "plank" in your own eye?

If you want to serve the upscale market, and particularly the Baby Boomers, you better have some respect for them. In most cases, they've earned it.

Remember this. More often than not, an affluent prospect is older and wiser and been around the block a time or two, just like me. With age and maturity comes an attitude – an attitude of intolerance. I'm much less likely to tolerate someone's disrespectful treatment of me today than I was in my youth.

And that's not just because I'm older now. But I've also attained a level of success where I'm less inclined to be tolerant of disrespect as well. And I think you'll find this is a common thread among the older population as well as the affluent population. Kind of like a double whammy, if you will.

Returning to the story of the magician who failed to do as he promised, perhaps because of his fame he was irritated that my daughter did not return his call more promptly. I don't know. More than likely he's just someone who is accustomed to the public adoration and ran up against someone who wasn't going to treat him like royalty – at least not in this situation.

So let's make a significant distinction right now between trust and respect.

> **Trust** is an honor that is given to you because of what you are expected to do in the future. **Respect,** however, is an honor that is given to you for what you are doing in the moment. Remember, however, that both trust and respect are based on "past" as well as "present" behavior.
>
> As a stager or re-designer, you trust them to give you the answers to the questions you will have for them and to pay you for your services when you are done. But how you treat them right now and throughout the process will tell them whether you also respect them.
>
> The same is true in reverse. They hopefully will trust you to deliver all of the goods and services you promise to them in the time frame that you promise – your future actions.
>
> But how they treat you right now shows whether they respect you or not.

Earning Their Respect

Everyone has a behavioral style. You do. I do. So does everyone else. Part of your job as a stager or re-designer is to quickly ascertain what style your prospect has so that you can adapt yours to theirs.

This is important, because once the emotions start to recede and rational decision-making starts to come into play, your success will be determined by how well you adapt.

There are 4 essential styles to consider:

1. **The Communicator** – These people like to influence others. They tend to dislike conflict. They will want to influence you into meeting their needs personally. They will seek out a good relationship and once they find it, you'll find that they can make quick decisions. You should find them easier to please because they won't hesitate to fully explain their expectations.
2. **The Controller** – This person requires organization and proof. They may want proof of the proof of the proof, so to speak.

They spend a lot of time looking over details and tend to be perfectionists, and they'll probably need more time to make decisions. So they will scrutinize you more throughout the whole process, particularly in the beginning.

3. **The Planner** – This person likes to work in advance, developing a plan for everything. So this person will also want to see that you can plan in advance and will be particularly interested in your process. When they are convinced that you have a specific process that makes sense, they will make a decision.

4. **The Actor** – I'm not referring to the movies, but I'm referring to someone who is a "doer". This personality style likes to take charge of things and they don't like it if they think you are wasting their time. They relish new opportunities and challenges. They might want to know more about the probabilities of a quick, profitable sale or the probabilities of finding a solution to an arrangement dilemma. Once they can see how you can definitely benefit them, they will make a quick decision.

To win someone's respect, you need to demonstrate your expertise. That is one of the reasons I have hundreds of free tips pages on my website, loaded with tips and images and such. It's also one of the reasons I offer so many options and so many products and services, so that any visitor to my site will know for certain that they have arrived at a company that not only offers real value, but has the expertise to back up any and all promises made.

People are primarily seeking solutions. It doesn't mean a whole heck of a lot if you have expertise if you don't know how to apply that expertise to individual situations. This is one of the reasons why our certification program is so excellent over other programs out there. We require our applicants to pass an exam to prove to us that they know the design theory and concepts and that they understand them.

After they pass the exam, they have to submit a portfolio to prove that they know how to **apply** the concepts in the real world. This is quite different from someone attending a seminar and being so-called "accredited" after 3 days. We think certification should require a whole lot more than attendance at a class or seminar or simply making a purchase of someone's book or membership site.

If you want to learn more about our high caliber certification, see Chapter 13 of this guide. You'll find all the information and current application fee. If you're reading this and you're a Gold or Diamond level trainee, you are already promised guaranteed certification. If you struggle with the exam or portfolio, we will personally work with you to assist you in passing. We do not guarantee certification, however, if you are not a Gold or Diamond level trainee.

If you're reading this and you have successfully completed our CSS or CRS process, you are to be congratulated. You have proven yourself to be the cream of the crop. Your CSS or CRS designation means far more because you **earned** it. You proved you had what it takes and you've proved you could take theory and concepts and make clients happy by achieving what you promised. Not all so-called "certified" or "accredited" stagers or re-designers who attain logos or insignias from other sources are able to reach this level of competence.

Building Deeper Relationships

A national stockbrokerage has run a series of TV commercials that I thought were outstanding. You've probably seen them. One shows a woman yelling wildly at a kid's soccer game. You automatically assume it's the mother of one of the players. Then it turns out it's the family's stockbroker instead. In another commercial, you see a man on the beach talking about the dream portfolio for retirement. Then it shows a woman and you assume it's the man's wife. But when the camera pans back, you see the woman is sitting next to her husband, and the stockbroker is a 3rd person in the scene.

What was so great about these commercials is that in just a few words, it conveyed the message that the stockbroker from this company was intricately involved and caring about the family he represented. Very powerful. Without say so, it suggest that the stockbroker has in some way become "part of the family".

You can easily see that the company wanted to convey that their agents and brokers were caring individuals and vitally interested in the major AND minor events of your family and your future. And isn't this what building deeper, lasting relationships is all about?

Obviously, the end goal is to close a sale with every prospect and, if possible, over time get repeat business and plenty of on-going referrals.

So, of course, that means that you actually have to ask a prospect for their business. It isn't going to happen unless you ask. They're not going to say, "OK, please let me do business with you!" You have to ask and this is where many stagers and re-designers choke and fail.

But wait! There are going to be those prospects with whom you have to ask, and ask, and ask, and ask. I don't mean nagging, like your kid does to you. But I do mean you'll have to build into your relationship what we call "mini-closes". It will be a sequence of them.

My son hardly ever asks me for anything. While my daughter doesn't ask often now as an adult, there have been times in her life when she just pounded me, over time, and eventually wore me down so that I finally gave in and said "yes" to whatever it was she wanted. She was a tenacious tyke.

A study in the *Greensboro News & Record* said that the average number of time a kid must ask for something before the parent gives in is 9 times. In the whole scheme of things, that's not all that many times. So you have no excuse. If you want the business, you have to ask for it – repeatedly.

So let's break it down further.

When to Ask

The best time to ask the first time is after you have finally shown some kind of promotional literature in a face-to-face meeting. You'll need to look for some signs from the prospect to let you know if this is a good time or not.

Here are some common signs that a prospect is ready:

- You see them nodding their head in agreement
- Their tone of voice becomes more relaxed
- They lean forward in their chair
- When you present alternatives, they express a strong preference
- They ask questions like, How much does it cost?, When can you start?, How long will it take?
- They verbalize approval, like "This makes sense" or "sounds good".
- They suggest a possible timing to begin that works for them
- They want to dig deeper into the facts
- They start to ask for your advice

- They comment on how nice it would be to work with you.

What to Ask For

What to ask for will be tailored to the type of service you are presenting and that they are considering. This could be to have you give them a complete analysis of their home. One of our 80-page checklist guides of recommended tasks is particularly beneficial in staging consultations. Or perhaps they are a re-design prospect. They want to hire you to rearrange their furnishings in a half-day or full-day appointment. Or maybe they want a color consultation or a buying service.

You will need to prepare in advance documents that lay out all the different options for them to consider that relate to the topic at hand.

How to Ask for What You Want

How to ask for what you want is typically referred to as "closing a sale". And if you take any sales training from anyone, you'll run into the standard techniques, five of which I'll briefly itemize here:

- **The Assumptive Close** – Use this when you can safely assume that they are ready to hire you. You'll find yourself saying something like, "It looks like you're about ready to hire me to stage (or redesign) your home. Am I right?" This probably won't be enough to actually close the deal, but it will set you up nicely for a few more questions and a firm deal.
- **The Testimonial Close** – Use stories of other situations to help you when you feel the prospect just needs a little more reassurance that you are right for them or that they will get the benefits they expect. You'll find yourself saying things like, "You remember when I said earlier . . ." This one is not the final close either, but heads you in the right direction.
- **The Succession Close** – Your questions in this close are geared to getting the prospect to answer "yes" to a short series of questions. You'll find yourself asking at the end of a statement, ". . . wouldn't you agree?" When done effectively, your final question should bring about a signed signature on your contract or agreement statement.
- **The Solution Close** – Never forget that one of the most powerful benefits of staging and redesign is that you will solve problems for the homeowner. So you can really use reminder

statements and questions to again pinpoint the problems you perceive them to be experiencing and reminding them of the solutions you will bring to the table.

- **The Straightforward Close** – Use this close when you are sure that you have developed a strong relationship and that they like you, trust you and respect you. You can even do it with humor, like "So stop dragging your feet and get out your wallet and let's get this thing done!" Once you've been in the business a while you'll begin to develop a sixth sense about which close you must use and eventually a certain style will come out of you that is uniquely yours.

Be Prepared for Objections

You always want to be prepared for objections as they will come up. Common ones will include:

- I'm not sure I need this type of service and can figure it out on my own
- I'd like to get a couple more bids on the project.
- Your fees are too high.
- I want to think about it some more.

No matter what "excuse" they give you, be prepared with follow up questions as to why they are saying what they are saying. Often times you just need to provide a bit more information to them so they feel comfortable. By probing more, you'll gain more information which will help you either proceed or return at a later date.

Here are some good questions:
1. Are there some other issues that we need to resolve first before you feel comfortable moving ahead?
2. Out of curiosity, would you mind telling me why you don't wish to proceed at this point?
3. I hope I haven't offended you in any way. Have I?

There will be some prospects that just won't budge. There will be others that need more information or validation or who need a price adjustment or additional time. And there will be others that will jump ahead instantly.

Being a professional stager and re-designer requires patience, understanding, strong communication skills and a bit of just plain straight forward blunt questions. Not to worry. You'll get your fair share of the action if you are professional, knowledgeable, have a positive attitude and are goal oriented.

Giving Them What You Promised

You don't have to look very long on my websites or get some of my training materials or free tips to discover that I'm a big fan of giving great detail, especially on the front end. I don't know any other home staging or interior redesign trainer on the planet who gives you such thorough information, to the point of being overwhelming, long before you've committed to buying anything. I have some people who call or write me and thank me for all the detail. I have a few that complain that it's just too much to read.

I believe in information. What can I say?

I also believe in giving what I promise – and even beyond that – I believe in giving **more** than I promise.

I believe in making my clients happy, at least as much as is humanly possible. I know there occasionally are people who will never be happy, who will never think they got enough. But they are the exception, not the norm, thank goodness.

But in the end, your business will live or die, thrive or stifle, based in large part on how well you promote it, but also by the degree that people are satisfied with what you delivered in the end, be it a service or a product.

And this is a critical point, because any consultant knows that getting referrals from satisfied clients is an important part of maintaining and growing their consulting business.

But no matter how much detail you give, you will find that people are notorious for skimming over copy and not reading what you have written. That happens to me fairly frequently. And as hard as I try and after as much effort as I have expended to give thorough information, I am still plagued by people who make assumptions that are unfounded.

While you cannot help what other people do, and while you cannot be held accountable for what other people assume, the better you can document what you will give to a client in exchange for your fees, the better off you will be.

 This is why, especially when it comes to home staging, it is vitally important to have some sort of written agreement or contract in place which you explain to your client and have them sign before you provide any services.

I have long operated a redesign service on the basis of a simple verbal agreement of what I will do and the fee I expect to receive. That is simple and best done, I think, with a "hand shake" type agreement.

But I would not provide home staging services with just a verbal agreement. You can do it, of course, but you're taking a big risk, because I guarantee you that you will open yourself up to higher levels of misconceptions and misunderstandings when the service gets more complicated.

In a court of law, there has to be what's called a "meeting of the minds". The more involved a service gets, the more difficult it is for both parties to be "on the same page", so to speak. So I do advise you to draw up a written proposal and record sufficient information about your proposed services so that a judge would look at the paperwork and feel that there was, indeed, a meeting of the minds.

For such a document, I recommend you see an attorney who is knowledgeable about the laws of your State and local community.

Whatever you agree to provide on your document, make sure you do everything you say you will do, do everything you wrote you would do and even go beyond that – do more than you promised. If you do that consistently, I can pretty well guarantee you that you will have very happy clients who will be more than happy to refer you to other people they know that might be interested in your services.
There is concrete evidence that shows that it takes five times the cost to land a new client than it does to garner the loyalty of an existing one. Your satisfied client should be expected to provide four critical things:

1. Use your services themselves in the future
2. Consider buying new products you offer in the future
3. Resist going to a competitor for similar services or products
4. Give you solicited and unsolicited referrals

So that makes them a valuable asset to your business.

Look for Wisdom Everywhere

Some of the best wisdom and training I've received personally has come from people who aren't in my industry at all. If you look for it, you're sure to find gems out there who can impart ideas and concepts that can be applied to decorating and design. You can even learn a lot by studying commercials on TV. Commercials must tell a story in 10, 15 or 30 seconds. Not much time at all.

Some are clever. An alarming number are absolutely stupid. Some are insulting. Some are extra informative. Some leave you totally hanging, wondering what just happened and why. But regardless of the type of commercial or the product or service being advertised, you can teach yourself a lot about conventional advertising.

I'm not especially promoting conventional advertising as a method for reaching the upscale market, or any market at all as a stager or re-designer. But one thing you will learn: how to boil your message down to the barest of essentials. You need to be able to do that effectively or you'll never be able to capture someone's interest when you first meet them.

Chapter 7
How to Attract the Affluent

Your Personal Appearance

If you want to attract the upscale client, you must look successful. It's a fact of life that we all "judge a book by its cover". So you need to "look" successful in order for people to assume you have the professional talent to serve them in the manner they expect. By looking successful, I mean your attire, your physical form (hair, makeup, grooming), your sales or work kit and your vehicle. Literally anything the client sees related to you, including your business card, literature and website.

I'm constantly amazed at the atrocious ways that people dress out in public - especially those that are overweight. And I don't care what someone's income level might be, there is no excuse for the way some people dress. I'm not talking about the expense of an outfit - I'm talking about the style.

Shocking to me, many, many overweight women today are wearing tight-fitted shirts and pants that accentuate every roll of fat on their mid bodies. Some are even rude enough to force the rest of the public to have to look at their belly bulging out under the shirt. Or we have to look at their too tight pants riding up on there lower abdomen, displaying all of the creases of their pelvic area, even the cellulite on their stomach, buttocks and thighs. This is very unprofessional and unappealing. I would never, ever consider hiring a person to do anything for me if they were dressed in such a manner or even anything closely remote to it.

Where has common sense gone? I myself have a weight issue (no, this isn't me), so I can relate to the frustrations of finding clothing that is suitable for my size, but I never would dress in a manner that obviously displays my weight in a distasteful manner. All of my clothing is loose and used to camouflage those areas of my body that need to be de-emphasized. I look for clothing that makes me look thinner and taller (lots of black) and I dress up my outfits with great looking accessories. Notice I said "great looking". I'm not talking about expensive accessories - but accessories that look great and are within my budget. Wouldn't you agree that this woman totally looks professional? I would hire her in a flash if I had a need for her service, whether I knew anything about her background and experience or not.

You see what people "buy" first is YOU - or rather, their perception of you. Nothing speaks more quickly to their perception as the manner in which you have "packaged" yourself: your wardrobe style, your makeup, your hairstyle, your nails, your shoes, your handbag, your carrying case. Did I say anything about the cost of anything? No. It's not necessarily how much you pay for your "package", but your choice of what you put together to make up the overall look.

If your hair is fabulous and you have put on your makeup perfectly, it will be of no help to you if you are dressed inappropriately. If you are dressed appropriately, but your nails are filthy, your nail polish is chipped and your hair is messed up, your wardrobe isn't going to save you. You've got to pay attention to every part of your total "package". Every element must be in place and must support the other elements. If one is not correct, the whole effect is ruined and may cost you lost business.

Quite naturally, people of all income brackets tend to socialize with people in their own economic bracket who tend to look like them, dress like them, act like them and so forth. They also tend to evaluate everyone else by the standard they place on themselves and that they see their friends living by. So there is going to be an automatic assumption on their part that someone who looks successful is someone who knows what they are doing. I'm that way. Bet you are too.

Professional Etiquette

A house guest arrived to spend a few days with a family. She was the adult daughter (40 years/single) of one of the parent's in the family. She had never met the other members of the family before. Within 5 minutes of arrival, she had proceeded to tell everyone that she was a very outspoken person, has gotten into trouble for doing so in the past and how she goes about engaging people she meets in conversations, by asking questions. Nothing novel about that. Within the next few minutes, she proceeds to insult the 24 years old daughter in front of her parents and other friends. An hour later, when the parents are not in the room, she chastises the 24 year old daughter regarding the daughter's chosen profession and the daughter's choice of boyfriend. Before and after the meals, she let's everyone else help with meal preparation and clean up, expecting to be waited on by her new "servants". While she had been very talkative before the meal, to the point of sermonizing to everyone, when she sits down to eat, she spends 97% of the time looking down at her plate, eating quietly, sometimes playing with her food, not joining in the conversation at all, and not even looking at other members of the family when they are speaking. It is not known whether she has ever received etiquette training or not, but my opinion is that there are many things in life one should just inherently KNOW and not have to be taught. Unless you are in someone's home as a trusted adviser, consultant, stager, re-designer or what have you, keep your opinions to yourself. Offer to help whenever tasks need to be done. Even if your help is not accepted, you must at least offer to help. When you attend parties, remember that you are there as a guest, but you should also be there to serve the hostess/host and their guests. Part of building a successful business is the ability to and desire to help other people. Never lose sight of that.

Other Tips on Image

Here are some tips for improving your physical appearance. Like it or not, people will judge each of us on our appearance and whether we "look" like a professional in our industry.

- Wear a suit or dress whenever possible. If you're not sure what to wear, wear a suit or dress, or pant suit.
- Some colors inspire trust more than others. Dark blue, for instance, tends to make people trust you more. Black, my favorite color, might not make a good choice because it tends to project an air of authority, which might not be best for the first meeting. Save black for the negotiating or consultation after they have hired you.
- Make sure all clothing is clean and pressed. Choose fabrics that do not wrinkle. For this reason I never wear linen, or satin for that matter. Make sure all clothing is new or looks new.
- Men might want to shave off the beards and mustaches. Many people are suspicious of those that wear them.
- To create the aura of being an affluent stager or re-designer in your own right, wear high-quality fabrics, leather belts and leather shoes.
- Women should avoid sexually suggestive clothing. If you are under 35, you need to dress older, so don't wear anything that looks girlish or collegiate or funky. Wear business attire.

- Look more to wear colors that are good for your skin tones. Don't combine several colors together. One or two colors are best.
- Keep all jewelry conservative and definitely don't wear anything that jangles or makes noises.
- If you are a young woman and you have a high pitched voice, practice lowering your voice. Little girls have high voices; women have lower voices. You will be more pleasant to listen to and you will appear older if you voice is lower.
- If you are an older woman and have an extremely low voice, or a voice affected by a long history of smoking, practice lifting the pitch of your voice to a more pleasant moderate level. Extremely low voices that make you sound manly can be a problem.

Other things to keep in mind:

- Don't be overly friendly.
- Don't be overly confident.
- Don't get too personal.
- Don't talk too much.
- Don't use profanity or vulgar words or phrases.
- Don't use technical terms.
- Don't get into controversial subjects.
- Don't criticize anyone, especially the competition.
- Don't divulge information about other clients unless it is completely anonymous.
- Don't fail to be complimentary when you can.

Your Personal Wardrobe Guide

Choosing a professional wardrobe need not be overwhelming if you follow some simple rules and guidelines. The starting place is to first understand your personal body type. Here is where many people get off track. If you're not purchasing styles that flatter your body type, you're not going to look as good as you could.

When appealing to the affluent, luxury prospect or client, it is even more important to look your best at all times. But you don't have to have a huge bank account to dress like the wealthy. You only need a few select, quality items in your core wardrobe. Here are some tips to help you.

Body Styles

Hour Glass Figure – Wouldn't we all like to have the hour glass figure. You can wear anything if you have this body type. You'll have a well proportioned bust line, thin waist, and hips in good proportion to the rest of your features.

Overly Large Bust or Shoulders – If your bust is too big (or at least you think it is) or your shoulders overly broad, don't wear styles that feature that area. Draw attention to your hips or other area of the body instead and that will help minimize all of the attention going where you least want emphasized. This will keep you from appearing top heavy.

Overly Large Waist – To hide the too-large waist, wear empire style clothing. This will enhance your bust while totally hiding the waist. Empire styles usually have a tight seam running across under the bust, then are free flowing from there down past the hips.

Overly Large Hips (Pear Shape) – Stay away completely from low rise pants or any style that carries a high contrasting belt or design running across the hips. Any time you have a strong horizontal line down by the hips, your hips will look even larger. Draw attention away from the hips.

Totally Skinny – Choose bright colors, lots of horizontal stripes, contrasting colors – this will help add a few visual pounds to your frame. Avoid wearing all one color, especially if it is black or some other dark color.

Totally Heavy All Over – Wear one color from top to bottom, preferably black or some other dark color. Avoid like the plague anything with horizontal lines and never wear one color on top with another strong color on the bottom. This will visually cut you in half making you look even wider. Never wear low rise pants and never wear pants or skirts that make you bulge out over the top

103

of them. Your clothing should be loose fitting at all times. If you wear skin tight clothing, it will make you look even heavier by drawing attention to bulges and folds of skin.

Core Clothing for Women

Here is a brief list of some core clothing that should be part of every woman's wardrobe.

- 3 Piece Suit -- Try a jacket, shirt and pants/skirt in a solid color.
- Navy Blazer -- A must have that makes an impression. Always in.
- White Shirt -- Nothing beats a crisp cotton shirt with or without French Cuffs.
- Khaki Slacks -- Versatility is their strong suit and they can withstand a nuclear winter.
- Cashmere Sweater or Twin Set -- Sedate or seductive. Your choice.
- Jeans -- Keep them "classic" and avoid low rise unless you're very thin or don't have enough hips. Dry-clean or press them yourself after washing.
- The Little Black Dress – The most versatile dress you will ever own. It works anywhere.
- Formal Attire -- Dramatic separates allow you to mix'n'match and make different outfits.
- Raincoat -- Go for a zip-out lining. The Trench Coat is the true classic.
- Pair of Black Pumps – 2" heels are sufficient
- Tie-back or Other Hair Ornament – When you're working, it's best to pull back your hair, especially if it is long
- Pair Black Flat Shoes – Comfortable shoes for when you're staging or redesign a home
- A Positive Self Image -- Nothing looks better on a woman than her confidence and pride.

Shopping Tips

After you have defined your style of body, you want to define your personal style. Some of you will be dramatic in style, some will be tailored and refined, some will like a modern "less is more" style and some will like a rustic, down-home All American look. Whatever you like, choose the shape of the outfit that fits your body type, or no matter how lovely the outfit, you will not like the results.

Choose the clothing that you love, that makes you feel comfortable and that expresses your personality. But don't be too predictable as that can be boring. Choose your personal style for your core wardrobe, and then try to add splashes of garments of varying styles to the core group so that your look doesn't become monotonous.

Look at your body and study it carefully for it's proportions, scale, it's best silhouette, what colors look best with your skin tones, what fabrics are most suitable to your size and shape. Choose only garments that flatter your body type.

Don't go on fishing expeditions looking for clothing. Decide specifically what you're looking for and stay focused on the mission, but don't be so rigid that you get frustrated and discouraged. Sometimes when I shop aimlessly, I stumble across something I just adore and buy it. And sometimes when I set out to find a specific item, I can't find it anywhere. Stay loose but try not to meander around too much.

Go to the right types of stores. I recently lost some weight and was in the market for some smaller jeans. Everywhere I looked, all I could find were low rise jeans made for skinny, young women. I knew I needed to shop in a more mature, conservative store to find what I was looking for. Sure enough, Gloria Vanderbilt had just what I needed. Try to choose clothing that is suitable for your age group, but if you're older, try to look a bit younger. And if you're very young, dress a bit older. Stay away from fads. Classic styles are always in and will always be considered professional.

Get plenty of rest before you go shopping. Shop alone. Don't look for sales. Choose quality stores when shopping for core items. Quality should come first. Take some nice heels and hose along.

Look first for clothing in colors that flatter your skin tones. You want to "wear the outfit" that makes your skin sparkle. When you try something on, observe your silhouette first. Fabric is the next consideration. Stay away from fabrics that show wrinkles easily, like satin or linen. Cotton is great when working because the fabric lets your skin breathe.

Buy outfits, not single units. This will save you a lot of money. Don't buy anything unless you are madly in love with everything about it. It won't grow on you over time.

Ask for help from the sales clerks, but take their comments with a grain of salt if they are on commission. You'll know who's on commission by how quickly they descend upon you to help you when you enter the store. Salaried only personnel tend to ignore you.

Insist that every garment you add to your wardrobe fits you. Get alterations immediately. Many of your finer stores will have an alteration service right there.

If you don't love it, leave it in the store.

Buy only quality items for your core wardrobe. These will stand the test of time and quality and you will always get your money's worth from them. You don't need a large wardrobe if you buy the right kinds of outfits. Remember that.

Other Tidbits

If you have large breasts, do not hold you handbag over your shoulder up by your breasts. This will just draw attention to them.

If you have large hips, don't hold your handbag down by your hips. Get it up higher.

If you have a small head or your hair pulled back in a bun, wear larger earrings. This will help put your head into better scale with the rest of your body.

If you have big bushy hair, minimize the earrings. They are not likely to show anyway and you don't want to add to the bulkiness on top.

Wardrobe Point System

To make sure your outfit is adequately accessorized, follow this simple math guide. Assign the proper points to what you are wearing and count them up. If you hit "8", you're just right. If you're under points, add something to the outfit to get to "8". If you are way over "8" total, start taking some stuff off. You're overdone.

- Open toed shoes (2 points)
- Closed toed shoes (1 point)
- Solid color pants/skirt (1 point)

106

- Patterned pants/skirt (2 points)
- Solid color top (1 point)
- Patterned top (2 points)
- Solid Color sweater/jacket/vest (1 point)
- Patterned sweater/jacket/vest (2 points)
- Earrings (1 point)
- Bracelet (1 point)
- Necklace (1 point)
- Hair ornament (1 point)
- Purse (1 point)
- Watch (0 points)
- Rings (0 points)

Avoid Negativity and Criticism

When a market expands, all segments of the market tend to grow in a similar manner. For referrals, this means, great customers will refer other great customers, whereas difficult clients will usually refer their equally difficult friends. Don't forget, you have a right to be selective.

Earlier today I received two emails. One was from a gal who had spent a good deal of time scouting my website and comparing my training programs to those of my competitors. She felt there were some red flags that she wanted to challenge me regarding and demanded that I answer a whole host of questions regarding my background and expertise, my methods and a number of other issues. While I'm usually happy to answer most questions posed to me, this gal was into "over kill", with suspicions abounding that a few answers weren't going to resolve no matter what I wrote. That sent up red flags to me. I don't have time for troublemakers and my peace is too important to me.

My response was a decision not to explain myself, nor to defend myself or my programs in any way. My response was, in essence, to tell her gently that I was obviously not the trainer for her. You see, while people have the ability to choose what I offer or not, I also have the ability to refuse to train someone. She's not the first person I've dismissed.

As luck would have it, within 30 minutes I received a second email from a current trainee, who proceeded to chastise me for my writing style, claiming that my books are full of grammatical errors, spelling errors, punctuation errors and a couple of other things I've never heard of. Sigh. Well, I'm sure there are some typos that get by me, and some other errors too, if you're going to scrutinize my writing as a so-called "English teacher of 12 years".

But I'm not interested in writing to please scholars or English teachers. I write the way I speak - personalized - frank - genuinely honest - grammatically twisted (sometimes). I write the way many mainstream American speaks. And I have plenty of people who write me and thank me - who say they felt I was sitting across the table and just talking to them and that it was easy to understand what I was communicating and they appreciated how personalized I made them feel.

And my style sells. What can I say?

Instead of attacking me with her superior attitude, she should have been paying attention to "how" I market and educate - because my success proves that, while I may not win any essay contests, I know how to be successful. And I know how to motivate people and encourage people.

People amaze me. Why would you go and bite the hand that feeds you? Not too smart. She didn't warrant a response at all.

The Unpleasant Into Opportunities

Life will occasionally hand you lemons. It's inevitable. I'll go for months without a single negative criticism. Then all of a sudden there's one. And I may get a small batch once in a great while.

I recently updated the file for my book "Advanced Redesign" and ordered more books to be printed. But when they arrived, I discovered the printer had used the older file instead of the newer one. What to do?

I could have written and chastised him and told him he was unprofessional and been very irate. But I wouldn't think of such a thing. I've learned a long time ago that it's much better to handle such situations softly, not with a mean spirit. Anyone can make a mistake.

I merely expressed disappointment. I did not ask for a reprint, though I was well within my rights to do so.

A day later, I not only got a very apologetic email back, but the promise that he would reprint the entire order and ship to me at no charge. And that is exactly what he did. So I wound up with twice the number of books I had ordered, which reduced my cost by more than half. Because of his error, I actually found myself in a slightly better situation than if there had been no error at all.

The same week, another printer I used also made an error. He too replaced the order and I got twice the product for the same money.

Try to look on every set back as a way to better your business. Many clouds have silver linings, they really do. Look how I've taken the two negative emails I received yesterday and turned them into something positive. I've used them as examples of what NOT to do. This helps you. Learn from the mistakes that other people make as well as the successes you see modeled around you. Learn from your own mistakes. And lighten up. Life is too short to be rude or critical or disrespectful.

Age might not reward with wealth, but it usually brings wisdom. Young people would do well to remember that and take advantage of the experience of older people. Look around you. You're probably surrounded by retired entrepreneurs who would be happy to mentor you at no charge. Take advantage of their experience.

The First 4 Minutes

I've already discussed the importance of first impressions. Just as curb appeal is part of creating the best first impression for a buyer of a home on the market, so too is the "face-to-face" appeal when you first meet a prospect. So here are a few good tips to help you prepare for a face-to-face meeting with a stranger, even if you've talked to the person over the phone or by email.

- Work out your "elevator speech" in advance. Practice it. You don't want to be caught off guard with no way to easily and quickly describe your business.
- Have a list of questions prepared in advance that will easily promote conversation and that you can fall back on if there are any "awkward silences". For help in how to hold meaningful conversations with total strangers, consider getting our ebook called, "Great Parties! Great Homes". It teaches you how to decorate for social events, but more than that it also teaches you how to be a great host/hostess for your own parties and how to be a great guest at other people's parties. Parties are a great place for networking your business, so this is a "must read". See Chapter 13 for more details.

- Look for ways to immediately compliment the prospect or find an area of interest that the prospect has that you can show interest in. Perhaps they own their business and you could get them to talk about how they began. Or perhaps you see that they own a collection of some sort that you can compliment or inquire about.
- It's important to treat the affluent prospect with respect, but don't act like some "fan" or "awestruck groupie". They may have large incomes or a large asset base, or even be celebrities or people with a measure of fame, but they are just human beings, not people to be "worshipped". Always remember that the best relationships are those where the prospect comes to respect you and needs you just as much as you need the prospect. Look for ways to establish common ground. Do not act toward them as if they are bigger than life.
- The reason you want to treat them as "regular" people is that you want to keep yourself from trying too hard to impress them. This will work against you because it makes you seem unsuccessful in your own right. That makes you look more like a mere salesperson rather than a legitimate consultant with a great deal of expertise.

Your Vocabulary

How you look is not the only aspect of your personal image that you must carefully scrutinize. What type of language you use is also an important ingredient that will either help you or hinder you. So here are some tips that will help you with the way you communicate verbally.

- Avoid all subjects that can be controversial, such as religion, politics, and sexual subjects.
- Avoid technical terms. Speak normally.
- Look for ways to naturally weave stories and examples into your conversation. Keep them short and to the point.
- Keep all facts and figures confidential by never revealing names. You can identify situations by location, but don't use names.
- Keep your own talk to a minimum in the beginning. Getting them to like you and know you generally is more important than espousing your sales pitch.

Public Relations

You probably already know that publicity is much more powerful in promoting a business than advertising – and publicity is generally free, whereas advertising costs a good deal of money. That's not to say that one should not advertise their business, but you will generally find that publicity will convert into clients better. Good publicity is more respected by consumers because they believe it to be 3rd party endorsement. By that I mean that an article in a magazine or newspaper or other source is viewed as an independent evaluation of your business by someone other than you. People tend to trust what they read about you more than what you say about yourself.

There are many ways to get publicity, but they all boil down to creating a "story" that the media think will be interesting to a wide audience. The media loves "news". They do not love self promotion.

But we're not discussing in this book getting publicity in general, but more specifically getting publicity that will be meaningful to luxury prospects and clients.

My business has been written about in Orange County Magazine, one of the most prestigious magazines in my part of the country. Just looking at an issue tells you it lies around the homes of affluent subscribers. It's got plush, expensive printing quality and the topics and photographs are very much in line with that assessment.

You'll have to test your various promotional markets and methods including:

- Self-liquidating seminars
- Booths at trade association conventions
- Appearances on TV, especially educational TV
- Published articles you've written for trade journals
- Speaking engagements at trade association conventions
- Interviews that have been published
- Marketing tactics to small business owners

But no campaign will be effective if it is poorly conceived or targeted to the wrong audience.

So your job is to figure out which magazines, which newspapers, which trade publications, which online sites the rich are looking at. Once you know that, then you can fine tune your campaigns accordingly. You'll find very quickly that the same pitch or offer will have differing results depending on the publication you choose, the timing of the campaign, the offer presented and so many other variables. It's kind of a science of its own.

You could decide to hire a public relations firm to design and manage campaigns for you. But be careful. You only want to work with firms that have a proven track record of reaching the rich and the affluent. Make sure you see examples of campaigns and measured results before you sign up with anyone. There are good firms and poor firms.

And sometimes it's not the publicity itself that brings the greatest results – it's what you do with that publicity afterwards. By using copies of articles and press releases that have been published to make contact or to stay in contact, you can extend the benefits of that exposure in a powerful way.

Writing Articles

Concentrate your articles and press releases in your local area. Unless you're set up for national services, it does you little good to go after national media. But what do you do if a competitor already has your local area "sewn up"? In that event, you're forced to work the national publications and trade journals. Then you use the reprints to leverage coverage locally. Hand out the reprints to clients and give them to your prospects.

You can always contact your local media outlets and just ask them if they will interview you for any upcoming staging or redesign segments forthcoming.

Be sure to set specific goals and challenges for yourself. Work consistently to build procedures and tactics geared to national and local articles, TV and radio appearances, speaking engagements at organizations, and appearances at social events.

Building Credibility

To help increase your credibility and generate more respect from affluent prospects and clients, associate yourself with credible symbols. One of the ways you can do that quite easily in the home staging and redesign industry is to apply for our certification insignias. We offer two: CSS (Certified Staging Specialist) and CRS (Certified Redesign Specialist).

Since you can't buy these insignia and the level of expertise that they represent, they carry a great deal of credibility when you display the symbols for this achievement. Unlike our competitors, who will so-called "certify" you because you purchased a seminar ticket or who will "certify" you because you purchased your way into their membership site, we think certification should have more requirements than your signature on a registration form or a credit card transaction.

That's why our certification program requires you to pass our exam and also requires you turn in a portfolio of example of work you have done. We don't care if you got paid for the work, but we do care to make sure you understand the concepts necessary to provide professional services and that you know how to apply those concepts in the real world.

To read more about our certification program, please see Chapter 13. If you are a Gold or Diamond level trainee, your certification is guaranteed. You merely have to go through the process, but if you are struggling to pass, we will work with you personally to help you until you pass.

Another way to build credibility is to associate your self with well known and highly respected organizations, like the Better Business Bureau. You don't have to do that right away (there is a sizeable annual fee to join), but by adding their logo to your marketing materials and website will help you in intangible ways that you might never know about specifically, but which you will benefit from over time.

To contact your local chapter, visit www.bbb.org.

Some entrepreneurs join charitable organizations that are well known, such as the United Way. This gives them instant credibility with some affluent prospects who are already members of the same organization with whom you will be working side by side for the benefit of the charity.

Other types of symbols of credibility are such entities as: your local church, your high school and college alumni associations, organizations like the Cystic Fibrosis Foundation, a local venture capital association, contacts within the FBI or CIA, local banking associations, national interior design associations and so forth.

Letters to the Editor

One of the least known methods of gaining some publicity is the process of writing letters to the editor of major and local publications. I know what you're thinking . . . you're thinking that most people never bother to read letters to the editor, so what's the point?

The point is not so much in the response to the letter once it gets published. This letter is just a cog in a larger scheme to get you where you want to go.

I for one do occasionally read the Letters to the Editor section of my favorite magazines or columns. Someone is reading them. Just look at the popularity of Dear Abby and other type of columns. You need to keep in mind that the letters to the editor are read by journalists and writers looking for stories and news. If they see your letter published, which always states you as the source, then they could at any time contact you about an article because they see you as a credible source for quotes.

But your use of the letter is not just reactive. It is also an opportunity for you to be pro-active. You can send out reprints of your letter along with related materials to your prospects, your clients, department heads, the media and so forth. To properly work the press, you need to keep in mind that it is a long-term commitment on your part to build a relationship so that when they need an article or a quote, they come to you for it.

Getting your letter published will give you instant credibility, confidence and a measure of self-esteem. Who doesn't like to see their name in print? The letter will also help separate you from "sales people" and give you a measure of esteem, so that prospects look at you differently, seeing you as a recognized authority in your field.

You can take a copy of your letter and add a cover letter to it that says something like, "Would you like to look over some of my ideas recently published in *The Wall Street Journal* or *Forbes Magazine* or some other prestigious publication?"

The mere fact that your letter got published says that the editor of that publication considered your letter of value for their readers. This is sort of an implied third-party endorsement, even when there actually isn't one in existence.

Also be on the look out for articles and opinions expressed by others that you can take exception to. Rejoinder letters that express opposing views to earlier letters, articles or tidbits are more likely to be published than any other kind of letter. I guess it's the element of controversy. We all know that controversy peaks the interest of consumers like few other things can.

So remember this one thing: A well timed, well targeted letter to the editor is more likely to get published than something that has no bite, no sizzle, no spark. Speak your mind. Then use the fact that you were published to promote your services to the affluent prospect.

Public Speaking

If the mere thought of speaking in public is enough to get your heart racing, you're not alone. One entrepreneur stared at his shoes while he pitched to the group. "[We were] having a conversation with the top of his head," said the group's leader. This will almost guarantee you failure. You've got to connect with your audience and be interesting. To help you do that, we've put together two Power Point Presentations (one on staging and one on redesign). We even wrote a script to go with each. The staging presentation has 65 slides and the redesign presentation has 60 slides (see Chapter 13). So there is no excuse for not making a good presentation for your business. All you have to do is edit the script to suit your needs and the audience you are presenting to. And don't feel like you have to show all of the slides or speak the entire script. The best presentations are more like conversations. That means leaving plenty of time at the end for questions.

Don't act nonchalant, however. One woman brought a glass of wine to the podium for her presentation. As the minutes ticked by, she became more and more nervous, and her hand started shaking. Eventually, she spilled the wine all over herself.

Whatever you do, keep your talk short. If you've just met someone informally, give them a 30-second description of your idea, and then ask if they want more information. Don't launch into a 20-minute pitch if your listener isn't interested.

In a formal setting, try to keep your presentation to ten minutes max - and certainly no longer than the time previously allotted by the group. Squeeze the most out of those minutes by staying on message and don't veer off onto aimless anecdotes. During one presentation, the entrepreneur couldn't help salivating over her dreams of appearing on Designed to Sell after she successfully launched her firm.

Don't overly dwell on your personal interests. They don't care how it ties into your love of window treatments, growing roses and so forth.

Do have professional business cards or postcards to hand out before the presentation. Pay the extra money to have your information printed on glossy card stock. It gives it a plush feeling that would make any upscale recipient think twice about throwing it away.

Speaking Tips

Whether you are speaking to a large audience or a small one, you want to tailor your presentation to suit the number of people and the size of the room. I once made the mistake of creating visuals for a small gathering only to find myself presenting to a huge auditorium filled with noisy Japanese students who were forced to attend. My visuals could not be seen past the first couple of rows and it was a complete waste of my time and theirs.

Here are some tips for preparing for your presentation:

- **Research your target.** Most groups gather for a common cause. Don't try to talk about interior redesign to a bunch of computer techies. They speak the language of math and HTML and won't understand a word you say. You'll just waste everyone's time.
- **Keep it informal.** Given a choice, many potential client groups (like real estate agents) will prefer meeting over lunch or coffee. You'll have to tailor your presentation for a small group who have a plate of salad and an entree in front of them, not your literature.

- **Rehearse.** Practice in front of business types from other industries. Yeah, you'll probably bore them, but you'll gain good experience and be "hot" when it counts.
- **Don't make them squint or squirm.** If you use Power Point slides, keep each to four lines of text or less. The slides should add color or imagery, not repeat what you are saying word for word. You'll find that ours have generally very little text per slide.
- **Bring a client if you have one.** Live testimonials from paying clients lend crucial credibility. Always refer to them as "client" and not "customers". If someone has truly benefited from what you offer, they might be just all too willing to come and speak about their experience. It's a compliment to them that you would ask them.
- **Ask for feedback.** When you're done, give your audience ample time to ask questions. If they aren't interested, ask them for the names of other groups who might be. Sometimes one person might be mildly interested until another person appears to be vitally interested. Then the mildly interested person becomes even more interested. Some people just need to know that someone else is interested before they can commit.

Conducting Seminars

A whole book could be written on this subject alone. Your first challenge is to get your prospects to look on your seminar as something other than a sales pitch. We're all kind of programmed to think that way and be suspicious.

To do this, you have to:

1. Target a specific area of need
2. Target a specific dissatisfaction
3. Make your seminar exclusive
4. Make your seminar "by invitation only"

To pull it off successfully, you have to deliver a well-planned presentation. You also have to spend a good deal of quality time and effort in building a great prospecting list. You can also team up with someone in a related but different field and join forces to reach the same market.

If teaming up with someone else, be sure to agree (in writing) that each prospect that attends will remain with the person who generated their attendance.

Now it is not a good idea to spring some hidden agenda upon them after they arrive. That will not go over very well. Make sure your seminar is packed with benefits that are incorporated into your invitation in advance.

Be sure to allow plenty of time for attendees to ask questions and get answers. Spend the extra time to get to know people. They will want to talk about themselves. Be prepared to listen. This is the time to cement your relationships with them. Remember, we're still concentrating on building lifetime friendships, not just one time encounters.

If you do it right, you should have about 7 opportunities to make contact with each prospect before, during and after the seminar. Here briefly are those 7 times:

1. Your First Phone Call - Make sure they know why they are being invited, what they can benefit from, that you understand how they feel and that you can solve their problems.
2. Your Confirmation Letter - This only goes out to those who accept the invitation. Tell them what it is, who will be conducting it, where it will be held, the start and ending time, and any other details.
3. Your Reminder Phone Call – Even though people agree to come, things happen. People forget. So be prepared to call them 2-3 days before the event to remind them. Ask if they have any questions. Get them to re-confirm.
4. Your Informal Reception – Try to personally greet each person when they arrive. If you can't do it, hire someone to do it for you. Be sure everyone is properly greeted and welcomed.
5. Your Seminar – It's better to plan for questions and answers as you go through the seminar rather than having it all at the end. This makes for a more interactive session and people appreciate being able to ask questions along the way.
6. Right After the Seminar – Have your appointment book with you during this time. Set up follow-up appointments right then while people are emotionally involved. People will expect you to follow up, so don't be timid here. Provide refreshments and encourage people to stay. Make sure you and your staff stays until the last guest leaves – no exceptions.

7. <u>Your Follow Up Phone Calls</u> – Call everyone you set an appointment with and confirm the appointment. Make them feel special by referring back to a question they had or some comment they made earlier. Assure them of your commitment to bring them great value and service.

More public speaking tips are included in my Advanced Redesign tutorial, which covers many advanced techniques for a staging and redesign business. You can read more about it at: http://www.decorate-redecorate.com/advanced-redesign.html.

Plan to use many visuals during your presentation. We are in a visual business and you know the saying, "a picture is worth a thousand words". Never underestimate the power of before and after pictures to illustrate what you mean.

Keep your presentation to about 45 minutes maximum. Psychologists know that it's very difficult to keep a person's attention for longer than 45 minutes. They will have difficulty remembering what is said beyond that time frame. The last thing you want to do is get people annoyed or worse, have them get up and leave.

Remember, the most critical time for you is right after the session ends. Even though you tell people in advance how long the seminar will be, people will always have other plans they try to include too. It's better to end with them wanting more, than to have them sigh and think, "Well, it's about time it ended." Leave them wanting more.

Being Prepared

Here are some tips on how to plan your seminar so that it comes off without a hitch. You need to try to anticipate every situation and possible problem in advance. This will be the most difficult when you first start out, but it will get easier each time you do one. So don't feel overwhelmed. It's a learning process, just like everything else.

- Scout out the location in advance
- Know what will be supplied for you and what will not
- Discuss your power supply: lighting, microphones, audio/visual equipment
- Know where the exits are
- Know what you will do in an emergency
- Be involved from beginning to end

- Set your goals and objectives in advance
- Know who will be staffing the event and their jobs
- Determine what you will need to take
- Arrive early
- Stay alert at all times
- Personally greet everyone as they arrive
- Prepare materials in advance to handout or to pass out during the seminar
- Have plenty of business cards
- Have an appointment book handy
- Have an equipment pre-check before anyone arrives
- Have plenty of people on hand to answer questions afterwards
- Arrange for coffee/tea/sodas/juice during the event
- Arrange for light snacks after the event
- Create a simple display off to one side where you place additional literature, business cards
- Get everyone's email address before you start, preferably during a registration session, if you don't already have it
- Hand out a brief evaluation form at the end to get valuable feedback – this will help you make your future seminars even better
- Clear your schedule to handle as many appointments right away as possible while prospects are most enthused

Attending Other Seminars

If you want to really improve your seminars, attend other seminars and study the tactics that other presenters use. Write down what you liked, what you didn't like, where you could improve on what they did. Notice the presenter's wardrobe, mannerisms, visuals, the way your are greeted, their follow up techniques, their offers, their call to action. The best way to hone your own skills is to critique others. It doesn't matter what type of seminar it is, you can learn from every situation.

But don't just attend to critique. Use the setting to network your own business while you are there. Here are some tips for what to do when you attend social events of all kinds:

- Know why you are attending
- Set some goals beyond critiquing
- Take a pen and tablet for notes
- Take plenty of business cards
- Show up early, ready to network

- Walk the entire room twice
- Note where the emergency exits are located
- Choose where you will sit
- Eat early before you arrive
- Don't smoke or drink before or during the event
- Force yourself to interact with people you don't know
- Spend 75% of the time you are there with strangers
- Hand pick 3-6 people to speak to specifically
- Shake hands firmly and smile
- Show confidence and be friendly
- Repeat their names twice if possible (the first time is to help you remember it; the second time is because they will like it)
- Be very brief when you state your name and what you do
- Say things that inspire others to ask you questions
- Give them your business card – get their card
- Get them talking about themselves (Ask them, "What brought you to this seminar?" This is an easy way to break the ice.)
- Keep asking questions.
- Listen always for indicators of dissatisfaction, their goals, their needs, what they do for a living, etc.
- If you find a need present that you can fulfill, suggest having breakfast or lunch the next day with them

But don't limit this process to attending seminars and social events. If you purposely place yourself in contact with other people on a regular basis, and by that I mean allocating 3-6 hours per week of being in social settings where you are meeting people, and you use the process above, you'll never have to worry about where your next client will come from. So it goes without saying, if you're attending events that the affluent attend, you'll automatically find yourself building a nice business with wealthy clients.

Guerrilla Marketing

Guerrilla marketing is all about efficiency, but that doesn't always mean spending less. Companies tend to allocate about 4% of sales to marketing, although some crafty guerrilla marketers may go as high as 8%.

The real investment here is the time and sweat spent understanding the needs of your customers and coming up with creative ways of communicating your value proposition. Broadening your search isn't as important as aiming your message at the right people - target marketing - and reaching out to them over and over again.

Offering free information is a relatively inexpensive way to build relationships with your customers - and to keep them coming back. That way, you become a resource for your customers, not just a vendor after a quick sale. For example: If you run a home staging business, offer tips on weekend fix-it projects or simple, quick decorating tips. You might also consider offering seminars on simple staging strategies - the perfect segue for selling your full service program at a special price just for that weekend.

A website is an obvious "must have". But it can't look sloppy and disorganized as so many of them do. Make it simple and straight forward. Prospective clients aren't interested in your past jobs or why you quit and started your business. They want to know what you can do for them. A simple tab labeled "About Us" that takes users to three or four paragraphs about you and your company is sufficient. They'll be more interested in seeing examples of what you've already done.

You'll also want to compile as much information on your visitors as possible. Include a question box on your web site that allows users to shoot you questions or comments or a blog where they can enter into discussions. This is a painless way to collect e-mail addresses of customers who really seem interested. Be sure to post your contact information in an easy to find location, especially at the bottom of your home page and on your "About Us" page.

Guerrilla marketing isn't just about having a web site. It's not enough to offer people a way to decorate or stage their home or hang art on their walls. Instead show them how a staged home will sell more quickly and for more money and how that can translate into their ability to buy a bigger home or pay off debts. Show them how much more relaxed and proud they will feel about their home when they invite guests over if it has been professionally arranged.

Spread Your Efforts Out

- **Polish your public speaking skills.**

    Local service clubs, churches, community organizations and special interest groups are hungry for speakers. Discuss the goings-on in your sector (for free) and weave in a soft sell. Answer all questions directly. If you can't help, direct the person to a competitor who can. Your honesty will be impressive and you'll find your audience will really trust you after that.

- **Write a column for the local newspaper.**

Run a brief column of tips about how to make a home look larger, how to get great curb appeal, how to romance a room. Even if your whole article isn't used, you probably will get some credit given you at the end. You can use that on your web site and in your literature to establish more credibility.

- **Send cards for no reason at all.**

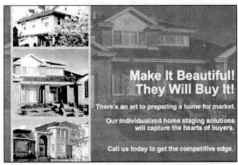

I hate it when I get impersonal Christmas cards, where the name has been stamped in gold by the printer or where the person just signed their name with no personal message to me at all. I'd rather not get the card at all than to be reminded that I mean too little to them to bother with a personal greeting. Instead, send out First Day of Spring, Summer, Fall or Winter cards. Or send out cards for no reason at all. Or attach the mailing to a customer's personal milestone, such as, "Congratulations on your daughter's graduation from high school." Whatever excuse you choose, be sure to personalize the message in some way so the recipient isn't left to feel like "just a number".

- **Go for the buzz.**

When not flying kites in thunderstorms, Ben Franklin pushed a wheelbarrow filled with paper to his printing shop to create the impression that his services were in great demand. Variations on this theme are endless. People are often reluctant to be the first to show enthusiasm, especially in a crowd. If you're conducting a seminar or speaking before a large group, have 2 or 3 pre-selected people help with registration. Instruct them to get up from within the audience and go to the registration table in the back AS you invite those in the audience to sign up for a special offer. Just the movement of a few people will help the rest feel more comfortable. You'll find it makes a big difference in the way the bulk of the audience responds. People don't want to be left out of a good deal and they tend to worry about not getting what they want when they want it.

I recently attended a weekend conference. At the end of the session, the host wanted to open up the microphone for a brief testimonial time. One of his staff members had come up to me an hour earlier and told me about this portion of the program. She asked if I would raise my hand right away and be the first person to give a testimony, explaining that it would make it easier for other people to volunteer theirs. I said, "Sure. No problem." A friend, seated in another part of the audience was also asked to do the same. He gave his testimony right after I gave mine. Then others started to raise their hands and there were no awkward moments during the transition.

Sometimes sales marketers will have "plants" in the audience. When the invitation to go to the back and purchase an item in limited supply is given, they jump up and go back, creating the illusion of a "run" on the item. This motivates other people to jump up and rush back to purchase the item before all are gone. These are all examples of generating a buzz.

You'll discover very quickly that people sometimes are sold on what they "assume" to be true. Most of the time what they assume was never promised or even mentioned. They jumped to conclusions based on situations that happened to them in the past. Assumptions can be both helpful and harmful. We all make assumptions; it just comes naturally.

- **Catch them off guard.**

Did you know that 98% of direct mail gets tossed before it's read? To get a 1% response is considered quite good. Instead of sending a message in an envelope, send empty envelopes with enticing headlines printed on the front and back. Pick out a good mailing house that specializes in "cleaned" targeted addresses of the affluent homeowner. Buy a small test mailing list. Make sure your company's name, address and phone number appear on the upper left corner of the envelope. A percentage of people will call to say the envelope was empty. This will lead to a friendly, low-key chat about the product or service behind the headline. Sneaky? Hey, it works.

- **Infiltrate the books.**

Tucking fliers or calling cards under windshield wipers is more annoying than effective. And, besides, it's hard to find a lot of cars all parked close together without also finding a security guard right on your tail. A better idea: Stuff business cards into relevant books at the library, a book store or at your local used book store. Every book store and library has a section on decorating. One company providing investigative services to law firms slipped its cards into law books at the courthouse library. Attorneys and paralegals assumed that other firms used the company, giving it credibility and causing its phone to ring off the hook.

- **Use a little sex - just a little.**

Well, within reason. One freelance voice-over artist played off the theme that he could work in the nude: He posed shirtless in a recording studio and used the photo on his demo tapes with the caption, "The Naked Voice." When I first published "Where There's a Wall - There's a Way" I entered a local decorating tradeshow. I took the cover photo and had it blown up to nearly life size and attached it to a sturdy board. Instead of the book's title, I used the slogan "101 Ways to Dress a Naked Wall" to garner attention. It grabbed so much attention I still use the slogan today.

- **Give out unexpected kindness.**

Customer loyalty programs can be expensive but with the upscale market, might be well worth the expense and effort. Include a small piece of scrumptious candy - it might even get customers to fill out that all-important customer survey that came along with the candy. Some savvy marketers have been known to put their business name and contact information on a small piece of paper inside a colored "fortune cookie". The downside is that someone might not want to break open the colored fortune cookie. The upside is that your message is definitely going to be read if they do. Who doesn't read their fortune?

- **Rev your engines.** A Harley-Davidson dealer in upstate New York advertised what it called a "cat shoot." This sparked calls from the Humane Society, police chief and even the mayor. Controversy always stirs people up. On the appointed day, the press and a large crowd showed up to find a six-foot high cardboard cat waiting to be peppered with a paintball gun. All proceeds went to charity, so no one cared, and the dealer got a lot of buzz.

  I'm a big fan of the hit TV show, "The Apprentice". There have been many episodes where the applicants had to create a "buzz" about a product or event. Naturally the more outrageous the claim, the more buzz you're likely to get. But keep in mind that the press doesn't like to be fooled very much. So if you do something that doesn't at least capture a laugh, you might get bad press instead of what you wanted.

- **Go for the Outrageous.**

  Sending or leaving something useful with your brief message can be great, so long as what you give away is useful. Desktop "pet rocks" bearing your company logo aren't going to do it. Why not pass out 12-inch rulers with catchy taglines such as, "How do we measure up to your expectations?" or "Slap us if we get it wrong and we'll get it right!" or "Put your stuff in our hands!" or "Naked homes don't sell well!" or "When it comes to staging – we rule!"

- **Pass Our Business Cards Everywhere**

  This bears repeating because so few people do it. Your business cards should be in color to stand out from the crowd. You should also have a brief statement of how you can help others on the back of the card. Wherever you go, pass out your card. Sometimes you'll get a card in return, but whether you do or you don't, give out your card. It's simple and very effective if done all the time and done over a period of time.

- **Join Your Local Real Estate Associations**

    I just heard from one of my trainees who joined her local real estate association and has made some important contacts there which have largely led to her staging over 50 homes so far in her short time in the business. The key to joining any organization is to go to the meetings faithfully and get involved. Don't be a wall flower. Stick your shy spirit in your pocket for the event and push yourself outside your comfort zone. Believe me, the most successful (and wealthy) agents and brokers attend these meetings.

Chapter 8
Selling to the Affluent

Give More Than You Promise

When I first launched my training programs on the internet, all of my competitors were selling high priced seminars and classes. Few, if any of them, offered a book (or ebook). Some would give out handouts, but many didn't even do that. So I found a niche and was the first to create an online training program of any kind.

I also have written extensively on my website about all of my products and services – sometimes to a fault – because I believe so totally in giving solid information. I then deliver exactly what I have promised to deliver – and more.

And so should you.

Last night my daughter and I ate at a local restaurant. I ordered a salad and soup. The soup was to be an "add on" to the salad for a nominal price. My daughter ordered the same salad. For $2.00 more she could add a piece of chicken. She didn't want the chicken and asked the waitress if she could substitute salmon for the chicken. She was told that could be done.

The meal was good, but when we received the bill, we were being charged full price for the bowl of soup and the salmon. When I inquired about the charges, stating that the menu listed other prices more reasonable and in keeping with what we had received, the waitress lied and said that there had been a price increase not stated on the menu.

Now I certainly could afford to pay the $9.00 overcharge, but that wasn't the point. You don't hand someone a menu, then charge them more for the "add on" or substitution unless you tell them in advance there will be an additional charge. And you don't charge them for food they never received, then claim the menu prices are not up to date.

Annoyed at being treated this way, I wound up speaking with the restaurant manager, who quickly made the price adjustment I requested and just shook her head when I told her what the waitress had claimed.

Not only did I leave the restaurant with negative feelings, that waitress missed out on the $10 tip I had planned to give her. Tips are for excellent service. I did not feel I received excellent service in this instance, so I was not about to reward her.

Give what you advertise – at the very least. But I say, go the extra distance. Give more than you promise. Most companies don't do that. As a matter of fact, most companies do the opposite.

I was just telling a stager the other day that out of the 7 independent contractors I had hired in recent months, I could only recommend the services of one. That is pretty poor. Either I'm doing a terrible job on the front end weeding out the good from the bad (which I don't think is the problem) or the average contractor doesn't know the meaning of service, integrity and the value of referrals.

Lastly, don't hype your services and give out misleading information.

I started this section making a comparison with my training programs and those of my competitors. As time has gone by, more and more trainers have entered some sort of online training program. Some appear to be honest and others are putting out blatant false advertising. Don't do that.

One competitor advertises the most highly "trafficked" website on staging. Prospective students are led to believe that the site is generating huge numbers of visiting prospects for a staging service. In reality, the vast majority of traffic is generated by some students, not consumers looking for services. The site also claims to have the most comprehensive training anywhere with a mere 100+ page book. Compare that with over 1500 pages of training here and counting.

This is a bad reflection on all of us. It reflects poorly on the industry at large and makes people talk negatively about home staging, stagers and trainers alike. Once a person becomes suspicious about one person in the industry, it's very difficult for them to overcome, even if they then meet someone with integrity.

Never forget that affluent clients and prospects network and have friends and family with other affluent people. Word will spread quickly.

So look carefully at what you state to make sure that you are giving sufficient information and that your information is accurate, full of value and exactly what you advertised.

However, having said that, if you have done everything right, and someone accuses you falsely, don't just back down out of fear of what they will say about you. There are times when you have to stand up for yourself and your company and stand your ground.

Periodically I have to do that when someone assumes something never stated or tries to force me to give them special treatment in some manner that is not given to everyone. I don't care if you're rich or poor, old or young, fat or skinny, I'm going to treat everyone with the same integrity, the same basic service, the same products, and hold them to the same terms and conditions.

A person might still go away angry because they didn't get their way, but I also believe my personal integrity is on the line. Once in a great while I'll get a call from someone who just skimmed the copy on the website and purchased a product, only to discover it wasn't what they assumed it would be. Some products are non refundable. Company policy does not allow anyone to make exceptions.

I don't take kindly to anyone claiming that I advertised falsely, because I don't do that ever. I have gone to extra lengths to give more than sufficient information about all of my products (even to a fault), so I will react aggressively if accused of doing otherwise.

However you decide to handle these types of situations is up to you. And while no business is perfect, you can minimize the possibility of this type of thing but giving loads of information and trying your best not to mislead anyone along the way. Enough said.

So be just as you advertise yourself to be. Be more not less. Be real. State your features and benefits and be consistent. Then you will develop a great reputation and your brand will become magnetic and highly successful.

Give Priority Treatment

You've probably figured out by now that affluent prospects and clients expect to be treated royally. They expect priority treatment, whether they deserve it or not. It often is something that they get elsewhere and think you should give it to them too.

So give them what they want –within reason, of course.

This is the only difference between how you should treat the rich versus the rest of consumers. Notice five paragraphs earlier I wrote, "I'm going to treat everyone (rich or poor) with the same integrity, the same basic service." The rich, however, are people with whom it's necessary to go above and beyond the "basic" service, not only because they expect it, but because it's an excellent investment of your time. Giving "extra service" beyond the basic service to the wealthy will result in repeat business and the introduction to or referral to other wealthy clients.

Everyone likes to feel important, but the wealthy person tends to feel they are more deserving of special treatment. And if the luxury prospect or client is also famous, they rather expect huge discounts or even freebies. I know some extremely wealthy people who never carry cash or even a wallet or credit card. Since people tend to fall over backwards to serve them for free, there is no need to carry money around at all.

I'm not saying you should give the rich a free ride. Far from it. They need to pay you and pay you well. But they have an attitude of entitlement that other people might not have, so you have to know about it and make your decisions in advance as to how you will handle them.

One stager called me up recently and was dismayed that a high-end realtor was expecting her to make multiple trips to a client's home to provide this service and that service. She had agreed to stage the home for the realtor at no charge, just to get her foot in the door with the realtor, believing that the realtor would send her other clients afterwards.

If you set yourself up to provide free services to get "in the front door", then don't complain afterwards if you feel you are being taken for granted or overused. That's what can happen, particularly with people who are accustomed to getting other people to jump at their beck and call.

You have to see the long term advantage to you and then make your decisions accordingly.

I try to treat everyone equally, as if every prospect and every client is wealthy. I think that is the best way to conduct business. If you set up your business in this manner, you never have to make decisions as to what to provide one and what to withhold from another. Always remember that some people are "on their way to wealth". They may not be there yet, but they're building. These types of people can be huge business for you - maybe not today, but in a few years.

Treat everyone with respect, honesty and great service. With the wealthy, it's good to invest extra time and effort to provide "extra great service". You can never go wrong with that commitment.

Your Personal Credo

Create your own personal "Credo". It's kind of a statement of your business philosophy. In Chapter 10 I'll give you an example of a Credo on service that can become part of your Credo, but you'll want to have some kind of company motto or statement of commitment. If you have an office that people come to, print up your credo and frame it and hang it in your office.

Include your credo in your company literature and on your own website. Don't expect people to pay a huge amount of attention to it, but do be aware that some will want to see it.

But more than that, it will help guide you and focus you on what's important to you and your business.

To be successful in selling your staging and redesign services to luxury prospects, you must be committed – wholly committed – not half hearted. You must develop a plan of action and stick to it, tweaking it as you go, but going with it.

Many people make plans, but their follow-through and commitment is lacking. They give up too soon and go on to other things.

Highly successful people never give up. They determine their goals and the path necessary to reach the goals. Then they steadfastly work the plan, day after day after day.

It is your commitment that will drown out that still small voice inside you that causes you to doubt yourself and your abilities. It is commitment that will cause you to work on those bright sunny days when you're tempted to go to the beach instead. It is commitment that will cause you to reach great heights. Without commitment, no business will survive.

Become a Trusted Adviser

I believe I've already stated earlier the importance of being looked upon as a trusted adviser to the affluent. Not only being a trusted adviser but even promoting yourself a "specializing" in servicing the more affluent persons in your local community.

There's just something very attractive to the rich about someone who claims to specialize in products and services geared just for them. Let's face it. Who among us doesn't like the feeling of being treated with special services not offered to everyone else? Be honest. You know you do.

And since the luxury prospect gets treated in special ways often enough, they have come to expect it and feel they deserve it as well. Happily they are often willing to pay extra to get it too – but not that you have to charge them more. I'm just saying they are willing to pay extra, so long as you spell it out to them in advance, that is.

You have to know they are savvy people. You have to know that they can discern integrity. They know when they are being misled – not always, but quite often. Don't try to fool them. They typically do their "homework" and research. They don't have time to waste and they don't appreciate it if you waste their time.

But if you do your job right and you prove to them you are trustworthy, you will become a magnet, not only of their business but to their friends and co-workers, who are likely to be affluent people too.

For this reason, you need to become totally informed about the industry and your products and services. But you would also do well to become totally informed about what your competitors are doing. By becoming thoroughly immersed in what's going on in your local area and nationally, you increase your client's and prospect's ability to trust you.

You will also be better able to give really terrific advice. Your knowledge becomes part of the value that your client buys. The more knowledge you have, the more value you bring to the table.

A Servant's Attitude

The whole goal we've been discussing is to help you not only start and grow a business serving the affluent members of your community, but to sustain your business long term. To get your first clients, and to initially attract all clients, you need to become a problem solver. But while that will get you started, it will only take you so far.

You've got to have a "servant's attitude". Sustaining your business requires you to combine being a servant with being a problem solver. This will help you get repeat business and that all-important word-of-mouth influence.

You'd be amazed at how important great service is and how little service is actually given by your competitors. Everyone wants to succeed but few will do what it really takes to succeed. Building a business, particularly with wealthy clients, takes a long time and involves lots of hard work. When you give excellent service, it is not only appreciated, it is remembered and talked about.

Service has become so poor with the majority of companies that if you provide it you will stand out. Add to that fact that wealthy prospects and clients are stressed out, you can see how it will be well received if you provide extraordinary service that eliminates problems and stress from their lives.

Solve Their Problems

I am the client of a company who helps me with various aspects of my business. They are very knowledgeable and the services they provide are targeted in specific areas. However, I had an area of my business causing me some headaches and I didn't know how to solve the problem. I mentioned it to my contact, who instantly jumped into action to help me resolve the matter.

He didn't charge me a cent. He researched the matter and gave me his advice. It wasn't his area. But he didn't care. He wanted to help me solve the problem, even though it was not part of our normal business relationship.

As a result, I am a very happy, satisfied customer. I would recommend him to others. I feel that he is working hard to help me achieve, and even though I know that my success benefits him as well, he didn't have to help me in this other matter. He could have merely said it was not his area of expertise and brushed me off. He didn't. Good for him.

This guy totally "gets it". He knows the value of a strong, long term relationship with my company and has proven he has my best interests at heart. It will pay off for him too.

Give Mega Value

Another mistake many entrepreneurs make is in the area of value. Price becomes an important consideration when you don't have value. Don't make the mistake of thinking that wealthy prospects and clients are not concerned about price.

It's true that they don't look at the price tags of small items. But they do care about price.

The difference between the rich and the poor is that the poor look for the lowest possible price. The rich are more concerned with getting the highest possible VALUE for the price they pay for goods and services. For this reason, they will investigate thoroughly the features and benefits of higher priced items.

If you've been around at all, you know there are always going to be a few people who will pump you for information and then go find the cheapest price they can get, taking with them the advantage of all that great information. Most affluent buyers will value the service, however, just as much as the price. They may even value the service higher than the price.

Actually, to tell you the truth, any time I get someone on the front end, rich or middle class or poor, who tries to grind me on price, I pass. I don't waste my time. I've learned through the years that people, who grind you on the front end, will grind you all through the process and complain at the end. There are just some people in life that you will never please, no matter what you do for them. So walk away from those prospects who are solely concerned about price. You don't need them and you don't want them, believe me.

Clearly articulate on the front end the value that your products and services will bring to the prospect. Stand behind what you claim. If you exceed their expectations, you will always have happy clients.

Eliminate All Hassles

I cannot stress this point enough. Eliminate the hassles for your client. Home staging, especially, is a time consuming service, full of details and specifics that can go wrong. This causes stress.

Your affluent client already lives with a tremendous amount of stress. More than likely your client works over 60 hours a week. They don't have time for problems. They don't like waiting. They want things done right the first time – on time. They are low on patience.

You want your clients to be loyal to you. Well, guess what? They want to be loyal to you because if you eliminate problems from their lives, they want to keep you around. They certainly don't want to have to hunt up someone to take your place if you screw up.

Work to make it easy for someone to do business with you. This is one of the biggest problems I face. My business and program has grown so extensively over the years that it is almost too much at times. My website alone contains hundreds and hundreds of pages, linking and interlinking to each other. It was a simple site in the beginning, but now, depending on your navigating habits, it can become overwhelming. I know this.

But once certain things are put into place, they can't be changed at all or are, at best, difficult to change down the road.

But we've grown up quite a bit compared to our early days. And you'll have to make changes and tweak your business as time goes by too.

As you add clients to your data base, make a point of logging in anything that caused the patience of your client to get tested. As you develop your processes, be sure to eliminate those areas so that dealing with you will truly be a hassle-free experience for your clients.

Get to know your affluent clients:

- Their dislikes
- Their likes
- Their pet peeves
- What influences them
- How they make decisions
- Their egos

- Their defense mechanisms
- When they work
- What they do
- How hard they work
- The stresses that plague them
- Their families
- Their friends

Get to know them better than they know themselves. Try to anticipate their needs before they arise. Do this and your business should thrive.

Back Up Your Promises

I almost made a business deal with a savvy business man. We spent many months working out the details and finally arrived at an agreement that was win/win to both parties.

He had convinced me that he had the expertise I was seeking and that I would be in great hands by entrusting some of my business with him.

Six weeks went by after I signed the initial documents to start working together. I never heard a peep from him in that time.

Finally I contacted him to inquire as to the progress of his work.

Nothing had been done on his end. I figured that was the case but wanted to give him an opportunity to explain his position. Instead of an apology or a reason that would make sense, I got nonsense and attitude from him.

He informed me that since our business transaction was out of the norm, he had placed me in last place on his agenda list. Even though he could have eventually made far, far more money with me than his typical clients, he chose not only to put me in last place, but to TELL ME HE PUT ME IN LAST PLACE.

That was a deal killer.

I'm a pretty understanding person and I fully recognize that things happen and things get delayed and so forth. I'm pretty reasonable. But to be told I would be last on the priority list was just unprofessional and, honestly, disrespectful.

And now I'm writing about the incident. He should be very, very happy I don't announce who he is so that the world could steer clear of him.

If you promise a prospect or client that you will do a certain amount of work by a specific time, be sure to do it. And under no circumstances should you abandon communication with your client and leave them hanging. Lack of communication and lack of follow thru will kill your business and earn you very bad press in your community.

When you are staging a property, you need to know that the people you hire to help you will do what they promise, when they promise to do it. It is extremely frustrating to work with outside vendors who don't show up on time, who make mistakes on the job, whose quality is inferior and whose service record is even worse.

So before you hire an independent contractor, get references. Check out other projects they have done. Talk to the homeowners. Check out their reputation with the Better Business Bureau.

If you offer a warranty or guarantee, stand behind it. Make good on all your promises. It doesn't take but one or two broken promises to make your client drop you or speak badly about your company.

Become Internet Savvy

Don't send out unsolicited email to prospects who have not given you permission to write them. This is called spam email and is against the law (CAN-SPAM Legislation). Collecting email addresses and having a website is important for your business growth. You can put a lot of helpful information on your website (if you own your own and didn't fall for those semi-custom websites promised by competing trainers). Information will help your prospects make decisions. Affluent prospects do their research online, so having great information on your site is important.

Unfortunately those people who have websites created by trainers will probably discover that the email collecting forms on their sites are being collected by the trainer with no way for the stager to collect emails from visitors to the site. These websites also will have much duplicated content and won't allow you to put up much information of your own. Images are definitely limited and so are changes.

Get your own website that you can actually own and control, one which will allow you to make unlimited changes and allow you to add as many pages as you like whenever you like and do it instantly without any additional fees or hassles. You won't need anyone's permission about the copy you put on the site either.

You'll find they are pretty easy to create with templates and quite easy to host, with fees ranging normally around $8-10 per month.

A web search for hosting companies will give you far more possibilities than you can dream of with lots of competitive hosting plans. If you're still hesitant about doing it yourself, get yourself a high school student or college student to put one up for you. They'll gain the experience and you'll gain your own website. A pretty good deal.

Make Full and Honest Disclosures

Yesterday I hired the phone company to install DSL for a computer in another part of my office. I had been told the service man would arrive between 8:30 and noon. At 3:00 PM he still had not shown up, but finally he called to say he was running late.

It was dark before he got done. I wasn't very happy with the service, but was glad it did get done.

Today I got a recorded phone call from the phone company, wanting to know if everything had gone according to their promises and wanting my feedback. They claimed that they really want to service me in the highest manner possible and are committed to that end. They gave me a way to simply punch a number to leave any request I wanted, but then the recording told me that the number wasn't working. So much for good follow-up.

So not only did they fail in their service promises on the front end, even their follow-up process was screwed up on the back end. This is pretty poor.

Here's another example in our own industry.

A competitor I mentioned earlier promises to build "highly optimized" websites for students, making it appear that the student will have floods of traffic coming to their little 5 page mini-site. One look at the source code on these types of sites says otherwise.

The trainer is registering "their" site in the trainer's name so that the unsuspecting student doesn't actually own the site (proven by the records at the WhoIs Registry). The student isn't told that a tiny site like this won't attract any visitors at all on its own. They aren't told that the majority of traffic coming to directory site (and then possibly to theirs) is primarily other students, not necessarily potential clients.

A bunch of the trainer's links are sprinkled all over the student's site, all pointing back to the trainer's programs, not to the student. The email addresses collected for newsletters go to the trainer, not to the student.

Students are further charged 3-5 times the going rate to host the site and are additionally severely restricted to just a few changes over the course of a year (4 in a whole year? Good grief!). And after charging the student for one year's worth of hosting fees, the student is locked in forever to the trainer because the trainer owns the site. So students can never get out from under the exorbitant hosting fees and take the website elsewhere if they choose. And if the name of the website is the same as the name of their business (a good idea normally), they will have to change the name of their business in order to get truly independent. And the tiny websites will never be expandable, at least not for the basic fees, which are already way above normal.

This reminds me of the web "malls" that sprung up all over the place a few years ago. The mall owners were charging $25 per month to host tiny little sites, claiming that they had a huge number of visitors that came to the mall and that mall participants would get the benefit of that traffic. Bunk! It didn't work then and it's not going to work now.

Would-be home stagers buy into these types of programs and only discover after it's too late that they aren't going to get what they thought they would get and that they were misled in many areas. Already many are vacating those kinds of directories as they figured out it wasn't the bonanza they were led to believe it was.

It's unfortunate for the stagers and they are easily duped because most people don't know what it takes to build a successful website and are easily led astray by their naiveté. It's ok to do this if you just want some web presence and you plan to direct traffic to your little site offline. But you'll never turn this type of site into something that really generates clients. It may happen for a few lucky ones once in a while, but it is not a good business model for the average person.

I tell you this so that you won't make this type of mistake when promoting your business to others. It isn't worth it in the end. Word gets around, particularly in businesses that are borne, bred and nurtured locally. You can't afford to have prospects and clients speak negatively about you, particularly when it comes to what you advertised.

Remember the earlier example of the restaurant who overcharged me? My point to the manager was that if the foods we ordered were going to be different from what was listed on the menu, if we were going to be charged extra for substitutions, we should have been informed at the time we placed the order. We should not have found out about the extra charges AFTER we ate the food and were ready to leave.

And we most certainly should **not** have been lied to as a cover-up when we challenged the waitress.

The vast majority of healthy, thriving businesses are owned by people who have made a commitment to it, who have made honest claims about their services and products, who work at it, who have developed professional attitudes and behaviors, who back up their promises with true, lasting value.

You will not last in business, or at least you will never truly excel in business, by sitting on the sidelines, by exaggerating benefits, by overcharging, by lying, by giving poor service and by having inferior products. It is bad enough to do so with the general public. It is suicide to do so in the affluent market.

The Buck Stops With You

As you've probably figured out by now, I'm a big believer in autonomy. It's your business and any time you give over a piece of control to someone else, you're not in business for yourself any longer. This is another reason why I'm against letting a trainer set up a website for you.

I've already explained that in most cases the trainer will forever own the domain name and address. Only the trainer will be able to make changes, additions or subtractions from the site. Bad news.

In the same manner that you always want to keep total control over your business, you need to understand that as a small business owner, you are the final word. The buck stops with you. You are the decision maker (or should be). So it is up to you to make good on your quality and services. You are the company.

You must accept full personal responsibility for everything you say and do. And to a degree, you are also responsible for service people that work for you or whom you hire on behalf of your client.

So you need to make sure every "team" member in your operation is in tune with the importance of offering quality products, superior service and full back-up in accordance with your guarantees and warranties.

Make No Excuses

Remember the waitress who lied about the price of the food in direct contradiction to the prices on the menu? She got caught and made up an excuse right on the spot. Bad idea. Very bad idea.

I once had an appointment with a prospective client. When I arrived at the location, my prospect was in a meeting and was not available. As I waited for her, another client in the building walked by and started to talk to me. This client drew me off to the side to discuss a product she wanted to acquire.

Next thing I knew, my prospect had ended her meeting and now wanted to see me. She let me know she was ready and I held up a finger to signal that I would be free in a minute.

When I got free from the client, I immediately went to see my prospect, who was "hot under the collar" because she had been made to wait for me. Instantly she verbally trounced on me.

Tempted as I was to defend myself, I instinctively knew that any kind of excuse making on my part would fall on deaf ears.

So I simply said, "I'm so sorry I kept you waiting. You have every right to be upset. I don't blame you in the least."

My prospect instantly settled down and got happy and we were able to transact business. Sometimes people just want to have you apologize. They just want you to acknowledge that they were hurt or felt disrespected and once you do that, all is fine.

Try not to screw up, but if you do, apologize instantly. If there is a legitimate reason, state the reason. But if there is no legitimate reason, whatever you do, don't make up a reason or try to lie your way out.

I went on to do business with my new client for years to come, but that never would have happened, I'm convinced, if I had made excuses or got angry that she was chastising me.

I admit that I haven't always reacted as I should in every situation, but thankfully I never made that mistake again. Mistakes are great motivators to getting your business in tip-top shape.

Remember to just treat people the way you would want to be treated and you won't go wrong – at least not very often – but even if something does "go wrong", you'll know you still did the right thing.

Never Over-Extend Yourself

There are few things I hate in business more than when someone promises me to get something done by a certain time or certain date and then fails to do so. Independent contractors have a notorious reputation for doing that.

They get the client to commit to a job, promising them the world and fast turn around. But very, very few of them make good on their promises. Do not do this to people.

Be a person of your word. It is rare in business.

I have several people I deal with on a regular basis that don't keep their word. I would drop them in a heart beat but can't find anyone to replace them with, so I'm stuck.

Home stagers and re-designers are starting businesses up right and left. These are booming fields right now. Don't make the mistake of thinking that you're the only game in town. You might be, but that's no excuse for not performing and keeping your promises.

So don't over-extend yourself by accepting too many projects at once. Know what you can handle. Know what stress level you can accept. Don't promise what you can't deliver. Word will get around about you if you run your business that way.

Once people start to distrust you, they will never get over it. Simply tell prospects that you have other obligations and that you don't want to hang them up. Ask them if you can start the project a little later. If they like you and trust you, they will probably be willing to wait for you.

Last week I visited my eye doctor for an exam. I needed new glasses. As we're right in the Christmas season, he was very busy and also going out of town. When I inquired about the turn around on the glasses, he told me honestly that it would take him 3-4 weeks to get them for me.

I would have purchased from him, but I didn't want to wait that long. But more than that, my respect for him as a professional went way up because he honestly told me he couldn't handle my purchase in a timely manner. I will refer other patients to him as a result.

He could have told me he would have the glasses in 2 weeks, then when the date came make up some story and blame it on the manufacturer or some such thing. But he didn't do that.

Be honest with people. You may lose a small sale in the here and now, but you'll gain so much more long term. And you'll be able to sleep at night.

Protect Your Reputation

Good word-of-mouth advertising is critical when dealing with the luxury or upscale market. Giving 100% to every project is the best way to win repeat and referral business. And even if it doesn't earn you anything, you can sleep peacefully at night knowing you run an honest business with impeccable integrity. Always leave your client in a state of receiving more from you than you promised.

Some stagers or re-designers seem to get all the luxury contracts; while others continue to battle for every dollar with lower-priced jobs. These designers frequently wonder why the other gal gets all the lucrative projects. The thing is, it's not by chance - it's by design. And that design begins with reputation.

The story of that uppity designer who got fired and the young design student who way over-priced her services will live on for years. And the story of how I saved the homeowner tens of thousands of dollars will also live on for years.

Branding, marketing and fulfillment all contribute to a designer's reputation - even more than education contributes. And it's that reputation that lands them in the lap of the luxury client - often without even having to compete for the project.

The definition of a luxury project, according to some, varies by market and designer. You can't simply put a dollar figure to define the luxury market.

Other designers say, "A luxury client is a client who considers great design, ideas, accessories and upgrades – with price not being a determining factor for these items." That's a pretty good definition, but this rules out the wealthy client who is a "discriminating" buyer, who is price conscious. This just indicates therefore the difficulty of defining a luxury client.

So the obvious question is: How can you reach the upscale (however we define it) and how can you do it without spending a fortune?

Consultants need to begin with their own personal brand. When it comes down to it, consumers are buying a person, not just a product. Look at how dynamically Donald Trump has branded his own name. The name Trump has become synonymous with quality. So a stager or re-designer is selling not just products and services, but reputation, talent, a sense of design, business acumen and personality. In general, consumers know they can get their products almost anywhere. So what the professional brings to the table is often the determining factor for who gets the sale.

You might want to pick up a copy of Trump's book titled "No Such Thing as Over-Exposure". It has a lot in it you can glean. Trump is a master at getting publicity and at branding his name, and therefore his business.

Stagers and re-designers need to create their brand by defining themselves in a manner that is consistent with the luxury market in their community and with their own sense of who they are and what they stand for.

I would advise you to build a relationship with existing clients - complete the projects to the last detail - and, within reason, spend money on your existing clients. This includes further marketing to them, but also sending thank you gifts.

Do not argue over an extra hour of your time or whether you charge rent for every little item. You can't afford to look petty. Newspapers get thrown out the next day, but the happy client will rave about you for years to come. I've been known to stay an extra 3 hours on a project without charging more money.

I price myself by the day and I take great pride in my work. So if I run out of time, you better believe I'm going to stay until I have it the way I want it.

As one designer put it, "You have to become your marketing statement and never slide for a moment. Luxury clientele expect this. They'll stand for nothing less." And time is what you do have to give. Yes, time is money. But sometimes the gift of time is better than the receipt of money. Experience will teach you this if you don't understand it now.

Someone wiser than all of us once said, "It's better to give than to receive."

The receipt of money is for now. A great reputation is forever.

9 Ways to Reach Out Yourself

But it isn't enough to have a brand that both the designer and the clients understand; rather, it's essential to be "out there" bringing in new luxury prospects to your web site or to your phone. Here are 10 more ways to reach the luxury market.

1. **Get yourself published** - There are a number of ways to accomplish this, from buying your way into some publications, to persistence, to good timing, to luck. Magazines and newspapers are looking for content. Every project has a story and the most interesting and compelling ones can get coverage, but you must take the responsibility to let publications know your story.

On a local level, develop relationships with the writers, publishers and editors of the newspapers and magazines. One of the most effective ways to reach luxury clients is through industry-related articles [that run] in a local publication every month with owner's photo and name."

2. **HGTV** - Like publications, HGTV is looking for content. With dozens of programs on the air telling hundreds of stories, there's no reason you

can't submit your own story and share in some of the popularity of design television. HGTV.com offers an interactive, easy way to tell your story to the appropriate producers, but in many cases you have to live in the area where they film the show. That, of course, is an asset to those who do and a disappointment to those who don't.

3. **Referrals** - The referral is likely the most common response to the question "How do you get new clients?" But be realistic. No one is going to give you a large, costly project without a referral. But do you use your referrals effectively? Are they gathered and used in marketing collaterals such as brochures, web sites and other advertisements? Or are you just waiting for the new client to wander in saying, "The Joneses sent us; they say you're great and that's good enough for us"?

Use your referrals systematically and proactively. Aligning your company with other businesses whose marketing statement and level of business parallels yours is essential to referral marketing. We have strategic alliances with money managers, investment firms, high-end real estate brokers and advertising agencies. The key is to treat your referrals as gold. Share the gold with the source of the referral.

4. **Design Awards** - Design awards provide your clients with a level of comfort that you are accomplished in your field. They build morale and pride among your staff. They provide genuine, quality content for press releases. They make wonderful adornments for your office, and they help position you as a credible and reputable professional.

5. **Networking Within Your Community** - Ever hear the saying, "It's not _what_ you know; it's _who_ you know"? My daughter is in the music business. Talent is one thing, but talent isn't going to get you anywhere because the world is full of talented people. It is, more often than not, a matter of who you know. Connections are vital in business.

People get comfortable and it's easier to automatically go with someone or something you know already. Networking is about getting to know more people: potential clients, potential leads, potential alliances, potential partners, potential friends.

You'll reach the luxury market by word of mouth with custom builders, architects and homeowners. You'll find it much harder to generate business from any other means, other than publicity or public speaking.

It would also be a good idea to develop relationships with high-end realtors, financial planners, insurance agents, plant services, landscapers and the like.

You can also create your own networking events. Host an event on behalf of the Interior Design or Architectural Associations in your area. Do one at least once each year. You can ensure you are in the forefront of their minds when decisions are being made."

6. **Get Involved** - Get involved directly through serving on boards, donating time and resources, or actively participating in a cause in which you believe. I've already talked about this previously. Whether it's your company, yourself, your staff or any combination of these, putting your name in the midst of worthy community causes adds to your brand, your name recognition and the comfort level you want with your potential luxury clientele.

Commit to be part of at least two industry related organizations to further your marketing statement. Consider involving yourself in such organizations as Habitat for Humanity. Support local high-end (private) high schools by donating through silent and live auctions at school-sponsored events. Buy banners that are hung in gyms supporting the athletic teams year-round while displaying your message all school year long.

7. **The Arts** - In almost every community, the luxury market is out spending a significant amount of disposable income on the arts. You want to be in front of these folks. Consider supporting the opera, symphony, theatre, ballet, music center or other arts group that draw a high-end audience. Typically the cost for support with an ad is reasonable in relation to the number of potential luxury clients seeing your name, your logo and your brand in yet another place - and this time you're supporting something they're passionate about. This creates an instant connection.

8. **Rely on Professionals** - Whether you rely on referrals, advertise in more traditional media or network to reach the luxury market, you must present yourself in a manner appropriate to the client base. So I say again, you have to "look the part". That means your logo, ads, brochures, Web site and face to the public should all be professional - always.

If you can afford to hire a marketing company, do so. If not, visit your local library and check out books on marketing concepts in the off line world as well as the online world.

9. **Words of Wisdom** - The designers quoted here feel they effectively reach the luxury market. Here is some advice directly from them.

- "Excel in quality. Focus only on the niche (and don't dilute your reputation by doing low/mid range). Respect your clients' time, ideas and, most of all, their money."
- "Repeat and referral business bring in highly qualified leads. So, once you have been in business long enough to build relationships, have treated your clients like gold, done exceptional work and built good relationships with reliable contractors, things will fall into place." In fact, 95% of your business can become repeat and referral business.
- "I see far too often with any professional that deals with the public's home front that they are intimidated by the money the luxury clientele has. They get nervous around money - afraid of it, afraid to ask for it. Luxury clients spend hundreds of dollars the way most of us spend ten dollars. You can not think of the money as money. You must, instead, stay true to your convictions and believe with your whole being in the design expertise you possess. Never put the money first or even think of it first. If the luxury client wants to hire you, they expect a professional, and they will accept the dollar figure that comes with your professionalism. They expect service and knowledge and the money is almost always secondary. All your marketing, ads, articles, etc. must solidify in their message that the luxury dollar is about service and professional expertise."

There is no one magical secret to reaching the luxury market. But in the end, it comes down to branding yourself to be attractive to the luxury market, marketing yourself to reach this market, and fulfilling your promises and then going the extra mile in order to ensure that they will be comfortable in their belief that you can offer the level of service they are accustomed to receiving and expecting to get.

Fine Tune Your Approach

Fine craftsmanship and the best quality products are "givens" in any upscale project. What will prompt clients to hire you as their stager or re-designer is your ability to understand their lifestyle and needs well enough to furnish them with peace of mind. And what will enable you to generate more business from existing clients is your ability to stay in touch and to listen to what their needs are long after the first project is completed.

Affluent clients happen to be good listeners when it comes to acquiring knowledge on issues that affect their lives. By tapping into that "need to know," you can create events for new clients who will also be receptive to learning about your business and what it has to offer.

Good communication is the key to each project's success. Building strong relationships need to be hallmarks of your company's operation.

Get Referrals

The reason most entrepreneurs don't get referrals is that they have no system in place to get them. In other words, they are making no concerted effort to get them. And they have no procedures in place to get referrals automatically. Big mistake.

People aren't just going to call you up and give you a referral. They might occasionally tell someone about you, but believe me, it's not in the forefront of their minds.

So you have to keep in touch with them periodically and remind them about you. This is best done when you give them something of value. It can be a little gift of information that costs you nothing.

Set up five (yes, I said 5) methods of acquiring referrals. You can do it by phone, by mail, from a website, from a newsletter. Use articles, write blurbs, send forms – whatever, but always ask for referrals from everyone. Make it a habit.

Do Unto Others

I know you've heard it before but it bears repeating: Do unto others as you would have them do unto you.

Life is too short to mislead people or short change them.

Years ago I met a young man who knew quite a bit about personal computers. He cleverly gained my trust and then proceeded to scam me out of several thousand dollars.

What was amazing about him is that he truly had talent and there was absolutely no need for him to scam people. He was just lazy and irresponsible.

Eventually I reported him to the police and sued him in small claims court and won. It took about 8 years for the police to investigate the case and for him to get arrested for felony grand theft.

He had to make full restitution and now has a felony record. He also spent 3 months in jail and was on probation for 3 years.

All that mess is a result of his choice to use his talents in unlawful ways. Sometimes I think about him and know that he could be making a huge income over the internet if he had just channeled his time and energy into fruitful, honest projects. He now has a daughter and an ex-girlfriend. He has ruined his life because he made a decision to steal rather than work.

Life will give you back what you give out. What you think controls what you say and what you say controls what you do and what you do controls the outcome of your energies.

So watch what you think and what you say and what you do. You might get away with some things here and there, but eventually it will catch up to you and it will do so at the least opportune moment.

Landing Upscale Clients

To get top clients, present an excellent business operation that stays on top of technical skills, avoid installation mistakes that cut into profit, participate in one's community, learn to communicate product capabilities, and stay in contact with the current client base to obtain a "branching" effect of referrals.

Here are a few other suggestions:

- Review your current client base, and focus on your best sales, including largest overall sales and sales that produced the highest gross margin.
- Likewise, focus on your best work, aesthetically, and the jobs which inspired the warmest client relationships.
- If you're new, this will be impossible. So practice on your home or homes of friends until you get some winning outcomes to focus on.
- Take a close look at the clients who you believe do the most entertaining, as these can be great referral candidates.
- Make a list of the clients for all of the above jobs, and put them on a special VIP list. These will be your preferred customers who should be privy to special events and the like, as they are most likely to bring in the kind of business that will be most valuable to you.
- Remember, when you're not selling your preferred client, someone else is.

Chapter 9
Pricing to the Affluent

Location

Have you ever heard the saying, "Location. Location. Location."? It's usually something one says in relation to where to put your business – the location of which would be paramount to one's success.

But one can use the same phrase when determining whether a particular prospect or client is affluent or not. Typically one would expect the rich to live in a very expensive home in an exclusive neighborhood.

While this is a pretty good measurement, it can be deceiving.

First of all, just because someone lives in an exclusive, expensive neighborhood, it doesn't mean that they have discretionary income. Their wealth could be "just on paper". In other words, their wealth could be tied up in investments for a long period of time.

If that is the case, they may be wealthy in terms of net worth, but they could very well be cash poor.

On the other hand, many truly wealthy people in this country live in very modest homes and drive very modest automobiles. So while there are some indicators of wealth on the outside, one really never knows if a prospect is affluent, nor the degree of that affluence, if indeed it does exist, until or unless you talk to them and get them to trust you with that kind of information.

Some people living in expensive homes are actually relatives or heirs of people who have wealth, but they themselves may not have much money at their disposal.

Size

The size of a home can be another indicator of possible wealth, but outward indicators are not always true and should only be thought of as "indicators", not fact.

Recently I heard on TV that the average home size in the past was about 1600 square feet. Today it is about 2400 square feet. So if 2400 square feet is the average, then if using size of home as an indicator of possible wealth, one would probably expect a truly wealthy person to be living in a home that is about 5000 square feet and larger.

Obviously as a stager or re-designer, when pricing a project, the size of the home will play a critical role in determining the fee to stage or redesign it.

The larger the home, the more furnishings there are likely to be. The longer a family has lived in a home can also be an indicator of how much "stuff" has been accumulated in the dwelling, not to mention the condition of the property.

Again, nothing is written in stone, but you will be able to gather some fairly good "clues" based on location and size.

Quality of Furnishings

As you would expect, the quality of the furnishings in a high priced home will probably be at a higher level. Not always, but usually. One of my clients, who built a multi-million dollar home spent so much money on the home itself, there was not enough left when it came time to furnish it.

So my client began picking up "bargains" at inexpensive stores. Some of the items were out of sync with the quality of the home and not ideal choices. This can happen with the "moderately" affluent who are inexperienced in investing, but for those who are the "extremely" affluent, there are usually enough resources to finish the job and do it right.

Whether new to affluence or not, there is sometimes a lack of understanding regarding accessories. Homeowners generally do not realize that their accessories convey their personality and taste. After the people who dwell there, accessories are next in importance in making a house into a home. Therefore, when staging, it's important to present not just a "house", but the potential for a "home".

I'm constantly amazed at the poor quality of accessories many people choose to buy. All too often they are very small and rather useless, especially when decorating large spaces. Affluent homes typically have large spacious rooms with very high ceilings. Tiny accessories just aren't going to do.

So to stage such a home properly, you're either going to have to have plenty of medium to large sized accessories on hand to "rent" to the owners, or you're going to have to have the owner rent them from a rental company.

Don't be too surprised if many rental companies don't have much selection in the higher end products. Do not, I repeat, do not put junk into a luxury home. It simply will not work.

Handsome slip covers can be put over furniture that is a lower quality, but accessories stand out there on their own drawing plenty of attention. They must be first rate or not at all.

When it comes to a redesign, however, you either need to go shopping for your client and purchase quality accessories for them, or assign them to the task. Some clients, who have few accessories, are uncomfortable with shopping for accessories, which explains why they don't have any, or if they have some, the selections don't work as they would like.

So offering a shopping service will be attractive to them and they should be able to give you a large enough budget to justify the time it will take to shop on their behalf.

Tweaking

Changing your rates can be based on the size of the home, the condition of the home, the neighborhood, your perceived evaluation of the client's ability to pay, and local competition.

You'll have to work with your pricing and it will change from year to year. Inflation alone can cause you to move your prices upwards. How busy you are will become a factor as time goes by.

The time of year and the amount of time you are given to complete the task can play a role in determining price. Obviously if you're pressed for time, it's fair that the client pay a higher rate than if you have plenty of time.

Fairness Rule

I want to emphasize once again the importance of treating the luxury or upscale client with the same level of service you would give anyone, though your delivery might be with more lavishly produced materials which they would expect you to have. I want to remind you **not** to up-charge your services just because you think they can afford to pay more.

Is that how you would want to be treated? I think not. So don't do it to them. You want to make sure that you don't under value your talent, time and expertise. If you charge too little, the client might think you're not very good or don't know what you're doing.

When you're in a bidding war for a project, it's ideal to fall in the middle of the price range rather than at the top or at the bottom of the scale. New consultants are often afraid to charge for services at all and tend to under-price their services as a result.

You have to strike a balance between being affordable and reasonable and not appearing so cheap that you are devalued.

I'm in the midst of hiring a landscape designer for a project. It will be an Asian garden for the backyard, which has to be blended with a couple other styles. While I want a Japanese designer, I'll not be looking for the cheapest or for the most expensive one.

Redesign Pricing

When I redesigned my last two multi-million dollar homes, I worked 2 full days (8 hours), plus a few extra hours each day to finish up (for which I did not charge). I charged the clients $750 for the day, which included my assistant who was there for part of the time but not the full day. If you break it down by the hour, it came to less than $75 per hour, for 2 people, and we got a huge amount of work done, not just for one room but for the entire home.

Would $750 feel expensive to them? Of course not. Would they likely feel that I had overly charged them or that I increased the price because of their income level? Not at all. They were thrilled with how much I had saved them compared to pricing they had received from competing designers, yet the price was substantial enough so that they felt I was indeed a professional worthy of working on their home.

My clients did not look on me as "cheap labor". At all times they viewed me as a talented designer who worked hard on their behalf and gave them the same pricing I would have given to anyone else.

My sister is a professional seamstress who used to live in Bozeman, Montana. One of her clients was Jane Fonda and her husband at the time, Ted Turner. As you may know, Ted is the owner of CNN and Jane is a well-known movie star, the daughter of Henry Fonda.

Jane and Ted were getting ready to attend a costume party and needed some alterations on their costumes. My sister was asked to drive out to their home, pick up the costumes, alter them and deliver them back.

To her credit, she charged them the exact same price she would have charged anyone - a fair price for her services and time. She was then delighted when Ted Turner gave her a substantial bonus.

It's far, far better to have your affluent client want to bonus you than to have them feel you have gouged them because you thought they could afford any amount you decided to charge.

One of the clients at a recent estate redesign gave me $250 more than I charged. And that resulted in an instant referral to another wealthy client. Had I overcharged her, you can bet there would not have been a referral. After I received the referral, I sent my client a beautiful thank you gift.

Be fair in your pricing, but do charge enough to cover your costs and make a reasonable profit.

Staging Pricing

The same philosophy should be applied when doing home staging. Balance your time, effort and expertise with the perceived value of what

you are providing to help you arrive at pricing that is both fair and competitive. Remember, there is a difference between "perceived value" and "true value". Prospects will buy your services and products based on "perceived value" but they will evaluate you later on "true value".

So you don't want to be caught short when it comes to "true value". That's why it's so important to learn your craft well by taking all the training you can get, particularly design training, and then work diligently to make your client – not just happy – but thrilled.

Since home staging is so much more involved than redesign, which can literally be done on a "gentleman's agreement", here are some more concrete guidelines that might help you with specifics, especially if you are drawing up a contract.

1. **DESCRIBE YOUR SERVICES:**
    o   Re-distribution of seller's home furnishings to maximize spaciousness and highlight home's architectural assets.
    o   Advisement of items to be removed temporarily which may detract from perceived assets of the home. Removal and storage of such is responsibility of seller or will be priced separately per hourly charge.
    o   Selection and placement of additional furniture or accessories (if needed) for up to 90 days. Additional fees to apply for extended terms and will vary according to

amount of furnishings provided and quality of furnishings.
- o Additional furnishings may include but are not limited to: bowls, baskets, candle holders, candles, artifacts, figurines, sculptures, containers, throw pillows, throws, framed art, mirrors, table plants, trees, floor plants, floral arrangements, bath towels, bath accessories, outdoor seating and table, lamps, tablecloths, dishes and silverware, linens. Installation services may or may not be included.
- o Large scale items may include but are not limited to: large framed artwork, large mirrors, large area rugs, silk floral arrangements, live plants and trees, potted plants or trees, bedspreads or comforters. These will be charged to seller at 45% of purchase price if provided by stager. Other options: Seller can purchase to keep or items can be rented from a rental vendor.
- o All rental of furniture and/or accessories must be arranged by seller directly with rental company and are not part of our services unless specified separately in writing.

2. **ITEMIZE YOUR FEES AND POLICIES:**
   - o A base price will be set depending on the square footage of the home and grounds. The larger the home, the higher the price. A home's condition is also a factor in determining price.
   - o The base price includes: initial consultation including check list of recommended tasks needed, a written proposal or booklet guide with detailed instructions and recommendations, professional rearrangement of existing furniture and accessories plus any rental furnishings, loan of additional accessories for up to 90 days, removal of loaned items at conclusion of term.
   - o Vacant homes, larger homes and executive homes will be priced on an individual basis and quotes are furnished at no charge and may or may not include a flat percentage of the selling price.
   - o A deposit of 50% is due upon signing of Staging Agreement with the balance due at completion of installation, **not** at the conclusion of rental period or sale of property.
   - o Additional services beyond the base charge will be added at the rate of $125-150 per hour with a minimum of 1 hour.

- Purchase of added furnishings will be 100% of purchase price, plus a shopping fee based on hourly rate above. 50% of purchasing budget to be paid in advance, with balance due upon delivery of furnishings and receipts.
- Furniture rental is between seller and rental company. Choose single pieces or groupings by the room. Rentals are normally for 2-3 month period, with delivery and pick up charges priced separately by rental company. Upscale furnishings are available for higher rates and recommended for upscale homes. A credit check and signed contract between seller and rental company is standard procedure.
- Damaged, lost or stolen items are the responsibility of seller to replace (at equivalent value) or pay replacement cost for items directly to stager.

Sample of Procedures You Might Include in a Brochure or Flyer

Describe the Procedures You Prefer to Use

We typically provide a market evaluation first, followed by the staging quote. Clients are welcome to use our services for recommendations only or to contract for full staging services.

By evaluating your property, we can determine what improvements or repairs are necessary to enable you to show your home to best advantage for a quick sale at optimum dollar. Our evaluations have a base price determined by size and condition of the property.

Quotes are provided at no additional charge.

Describe Your Consultation Services

Our market evaluation and our 80-page Home Staging for Yourself checklist guide (be sure to get some of these at http://www.decorate-redecorate.com/home-staging-for-yourself.html) will include detailed suggestions for the interior and exteriors of the home. We include color recommendations and samples to help guide you if you wish.

Evaluations can take between 1-4 hours. The minimum base price is $_____ and increases with size and/or condition of property.

No evaluation will be made without a pre-agreed price. Clients immediately receive a completed check list and a more detailed written report, with accompanying photos, will be provided on request for an additional fee of $_____.

Describe Your Staging or Redesign Services

For those clients who will live in the home while it is on the market, we offer interior redesign services. Your existing furnishings will be edited to make the home look more spacious and de-cluttered to allow it to appear organized. Furnishings are repositioned to enhance each room according to standard interior design theory and concepts and suggestions to buyers for alternate usages for the room will be made if needed.

We will attempt to incorporate as many of your furnishings as possible to minimize costs, however, supplemental furniture or accessories may be deemed necessary to complete the look for the greatest appeal to buyers.

You may choose accessories from our inventory to rent or upon an agreed budget, we will be happy to buy accessories on your behalf to complete the design. Additional accessories usually fall in the realm of plants, artwork, pillows and table ornamentation.

Describe Your Staging Services for Vacant Homes

Selection of furnishings will be made in keeping with: your style, your color scheme, the neighborhood and your budget needs. Areas of most concern will be your Entry, Living Room, Family Room, Kitchen, Baths and Master Bedroom. Attention will also be given to the front and back exteriors.

*Prices subject to change without notice. We retain a $2,000.00 minimum for staging services.

Typical Prices You Might Charge

Size of Home	Consultation (add $35 for in-depth Guide)	Hourly Rates	Your Staging Props	Rental of Staging Props
Less than 2000	$350	$125.00 per hr.	$200 - $1500	$1750 - $5000+
2001 - 2500	$350	$125.00 per hr.	$200 - $1750	$2750 - $6000+
2501 - 3000	$350	$125.00 per hr.	$200 - $2000	$3250 - $8000+
3001 - 3500	$400	$125.00 per hr.	$200 - $2250	$3750 - $9000+
3501 - 4000	$400	$125.00 per hr.	$200 - $2500	$4250 - $12000+
4001 - 4500	$450	$125.00 per hr.	$200 - $2750	$4750 - $15000+
4501 - 5000	$450	$125.00 per hr.	$200 - $3000	$5250 - $20000+
5001+	$500+	$125.00 per hr.	$200 - $3250+	$5750 - $30000+

We have a growing inventory of accessories for vacant properties which includes a wide variety of home decorating pieces. Rental rates by 3rd party rental companies will vary according to style, value and number of pieces rented. Luxury homes will require up-scale pieces that are larger and more artistic or distinctive and will be priced accordingly.

Affluent Clients Prefer Written Proposals

It's pretty common to charge a minimum of 2 hours for an initial consultation. Your service will include a detailed walk-thru of the home while completing a thorough check list of tasks you recommend. We have a fully developed check list of 25 pages included in <u>Home Staging for Profit</u> but you can also get our 80-page checklist guide booklets to help you with your consultations called <u>Home Staging for Yourself</u> (See Chapter 13). By using the 80 page guide, you can literally eliminate the need for a written proposal, but you can provide one if you like.

An initial general check list is perfect to hand to the seller upon completion of the evaluation. However, it is far more professional to personalize the check list with a detailed write up, including photographs of the home. Photographs should show problem areas, especially if they are severe problems. In our 80-page checklist guide booklet, we've provided ample space to write in specific instructions, either for yourself or to give to the homeowner who wishes to tackle the actual staging without your services.

In many cases, once the seller sees the mammoth task to properly prepare their property, as outlined in the 80-page guide, they might then elect to hire you instead.

If you also give a written estimate or itemization to the client, rather than faxing your written recommendations or mailing them, consider hand delivering them. The advantage of the hand delivered report puts you back at the home and in the prime position of getting the seller to hire you for a full service staging or redesign service.

Create a polished, classy presentation. It should be prepared on your computer, include a cover letter and placed in a presentation folder, along with your business card.

This type of proposal will impress the affluent client. I cannot tell you how many vendors I have interviewed on a wide variety of projects and the number of impressive proposals I have received. Many times I haven't received a proposal at all or it has been merely a verbal quote.

The vendors who have impressed me the most have been the ones who gave me a formal quote with detailed descriptions as to what was included, and who also provided me with copies of their business license, workers compensation verification, liability insurance and contractor's license.

When you consider how much work is typically needed to prepare a home for market, you'll quickly realize that the seller needs detailed information from you. Their agent will appreciate your attention to detail as well, and this will lead to further referrals and an on-going business relationship. That on-going relationship is critical to sustaining your business for years to come.

Give Some Advice in Your Proposal

Here's some advice you could consider including (from March Chandra, Real Estate Broker and Owner of Cutting Edge Real Estate in California):

"Are you thinking of remodeling your home? Consider the return on your investment before remodeling.

Not all remodeling projects yield the same return in increasing your home's value. Updating your kitchen and baths is your best remodeling investment, returning a nearly dollar-for-dollar increase in home resale value. An updated kitchen and bathrooms make your home that much more attractive to potential buyers when you do decide to sell.

By contrast, converting a basement into a family room or adding outdoor recreation facilities, such as a swimming pool or sport court, yield the lowest return on your investment. Sometimes the cumulative effect of several smaller projects can yield a higher resale value than one or two larger ones.

Smaller projects tend to be more cosmetic - new paint, doors, or windows. Larger projects that upgrade or add living space may cost more, but almost always add less resale value for the dollars spent.

Whatever you do, be careful of over-improving for your neighborhood. Remodeling that significantly improves your property over neighboring homes won't return as much when it comes time to sell."

Three Levels of Service

Even though I have laid out some hourly rates and other fees, and given you quite a few options, I believe it is in your best interest to also offer some flat rate options. Many people are uncomfortable with paying hourly fees because they are concerned about the fact that such an arrangement could be to their disadvantage.

I don't know about you, but I'm one of those types. I want to know in advance my worst case scenario so there are no surprises that might make me unhappy. I don't like open-ended agreements of any kind and there are many, many people who feel just like me.

Then there is the fact that some people will shut down totally if given too many options. If they don't know what option is right for them, they get confused and concerned they will select the wrong option. When that happens they may just decide the whole process is too confusing. That could leave you out in the cold with no money in your pocket.

So here is what I suggest.
Create 3 levels of flat rate services. The first level, let's call it Ruby, is your budget program. The second level, Emerald, is your designer program. And the 3rd level, Sapphire, is your premier program.

For the upscale client, you don't want to use terms like "budget" or "low price" or any term that suggests low income status. So choose descriptions that carry an upscale image associated with them. It doesn't have to be jewels, but just make sure the descriptions are suitable for the caliber of clientele and property you will be quoting on.

Ruby – This program will be your least expensive program. You'll need to calculate a flat rate for consultation of an upscale, executive type property. You'll need to calculate either a daily rate for anticipated services and factor that in or charge a flat percentage of the sales price of the home. Once you know the asking price anticipated before staging, you've got to allow for the fact that the asking price AFTER staging will likely be higher. A 1% commission on the final asking price should be reasonable and you'll want to collect a percentage of that upon conclusion of the staging services. The balance could be collected

upon the sale of the home. If you're willing to wait for your money upon the sale of the home, then a commission on the home can be quite lucrative. Any furnishings needed in this program will be sparse and more basic.

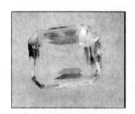

Emerald - This program will be your moderate, designer program. You'll need to calculate a flat rate for consultation of an upscale, executive type property. The flat rate in this program will be higher than it was for Ruby. You'll need to calculate either a daily rate for anticipated services and factor that in or charge a flat percentage of the sales price of the home. The daily rate or percentage you charge on this program will be slightly higher than in the Ruby program.

Once you know the asking price anticipated before staging, you've got to allow for the fact that the asking price AFTER staging will likely be higher. A 1.2% commission on the final asking price should be reasonable and you'll want to collect a percentage of that upon conclusion of the staging services. The balance could be collected upon the sale of the home. If you're willing to wait for your money upon the sale of the home, then a commission on the home can be quite lucrative. Any furnishings needed in this program will be designer quality and you will provide more furnishings than in the Ruby program.

Sapphire - This program will be your executive, deluxe program. You'll need to calculate a flat rate for consultation of an upscale, executive type property. The flat rate in this program will be higher than it was for Ruby or Emerald. You'll need to calculate either a daily rate for anticipated services and factor that in or charge a flat percentage of the sales price of the home. The daily rate or percentage you charge on this program will be slightly higher than in the Ruby or Emerald programs.

Once you know the asking price anticipated before staging, you've got to allow for the fact that the asking price AFTER staging will likely be higher. A 1.35% commission on the final asking price should be reasonable and you'll want to collect a percentage of that upon conclusion of the staging services. The balance could be collected upon the sale of the home. If you're willing to wait for your money upon the sale of the home, then a commission on the home can be quite lucrative. Any furnishings needed in this program will be the best quality available and you will provide a complete, high-class furnished environment.

OK, there you have some kind of guideline for presenting flat rate programs to prospects. Bear in mind that the details of these programs will be trial and error at first. You'll have to test them out. You might have to lower the percentage or tweak the program in some way. There are no hard, fast rules.

You may find that you got short-changed the first time you do one. If so, don't be concerned and think of it as a training project. Change it for the next client. Or you may find that you got overpaid and the client was a bit disturbed. In that case, lower your fees for the next client. Many issues in this business change dramatically from one project to another, so a stager is always faced with having to make adjustments. Competition in your area alone may force you to make adjustments you wouldn't otherwise do.

This is why we don't give actual fees in more detail than we do. There are just too many factors involved and our training is purchased by stagers and re-designers all over the country and in foreign countries as well. But I believe we have given everyone enough of a starting point so that they will be able to work out a program that suits them and that is good for the area where they live and work.

Upscale Marketing Materials

Collateral materials must be printed [on] the best paper, with the best photos, unique graphic design elements combined with the most excellent before and after photos. This is what it takes to appeal to upscale clients.

When you are ready to present yourself to the luxury world, be sure you are ready. Upgrade all your marketing materials to reflect a more upscale and professional look, and use a professional design firm to make it happen. This creates a comfort level among upscale clients that you speak their language and move in their world; it also goes a long way toward convincing them that you will know what it takes to create the kind of caliber project that they are looking for.

Your website should look first class. Pay a designer to create something for you or find a student who has learned HTML to put one together for you. Make the design clean and contemporary. Decide on a style and carry the style throughout your site. Choose colors that blend and look appealing. Make sure the site is very readable. I've seen so many websites that just don't measure up at all. I can't see any one, whether an upscale visitor or middle class, wanting to hire the owner.

Whatever you do, avoid the template mini "semi-custom" websites now being pitched by other trainers. They will do you very little good. They are too small to rank well on search engines, they are filled with duplicate content and might not even get indexed at all, most of the links head back to the trainer and not to you, they're usually registered and owned by the trainer and not by you (so your business name would have to be changed if you ever wanted to move the site elsewhere or make it bigger and better) or you'd have to pay the trainer a high fee to "buy" the domain name in order to move it to another server of your choice. There are just a host of reasons why that route is not advisable.

Many colleges and universities now offer online classes in web design. You'll even find community colleges offering convenient classes for nominal fees. Several years ago I took a community college class and that's how I got my start on the internet.

Having your own site and total autonomy on its content and size is really important. You definitely don't want to get stuck with duplicate content or the inability to make changes whenever you want or the inability to expand your site if you want.

I just got a call from one of my trainees asking me about creating a brochure. I told her she can go down that route, but I don't advise it until or unless you are well established. It's a huge expense and undertaking to create a brochure and once printed you can't change anything without another expensive reprint.

This is why you have a website.

Next, using your word processing program, you can easily create nice letterhead that is sufficient. Then put your facts, figures, forms, benefits and features lists, your references and such on clean, classy paper and print off yourself on your computer's printer.

You can go a very long, long way without committing to an expensive brochure. That's kind of old school nowadays. Select some quality stationery at your local office supply store, say something tan or grey or a bright white. Buy all of your paper at 24 lb, not the cheaper 20 lb paper.

Just having beautiful quality paper will give you an upscale image. We also offer exquisite promotional cards which have great marketing messages. You can purchase them a la carte if you don't want the hassles of making your own or if you don't have the know-how. Read all about them in Chapter 13.

Chapter 10
How to Service the Affluent

The Importance of Service

Nowadays you cannot sustain a business very well without great service. This is even more essential when dealing with upscale clients and prospects. They not only deserve great service, they demand it - and rightly so.

I stated earlier that the luxury client may value great service higher than any other aspect of what you offer, including a great price. So you better be prepared to do what you say you're going to do and do it when you promise you would and finish when you promise to have it done. You better do a quality job in a timely manner or you'll have problems. It's as simple as that.

Before I get into talking about the kind of service you should provide, let me first give you examples of what you should NOT do.

The UPS Example

My husband's company has been a UPS client for decades. In former times, to process a shipment by UPS, you were given a book to fill out by hand. You would print up labels with your account number on them and then just write the customer's name and address on the label. Pretty simple method.

But now UPS is trying to get every customer to process the labels online with a computer. This requires you have a computer and online capability in your shipping department, which is something not all companies have nor want to have.

Recently my husband moved his company from Los Angeles to Orange County to be closer to home and to downsize and tighten up his overhead.

But when he went to set up his account again at the new location, he was told by multiple people at UPS that he must have a computer and process online labels.

He refused. Let's face it. He's 67 years old, doesn't know how to turn a computer on and doesn't want to learn either.

So he got frustrated and said to them, "So then why are you running commercials that say, 'What Can Brown Do For You?' So far Brown isn't doing anything for me." After he got dead silence he then said, "Well, then I'll close my account and go to FEDEX instead." You'd be amazed at how quickly UPS changed their "policy" when he threatened to go to a competitor.

Now I don't blame UPS for wanting to move all vendors to computerized labels. It makes their process easier and I'm sure they've gotten rid of plenty of staff that used to be required, but still it's not a good idea to totally annoy a long standing customer by being inflexible.

This inflexibility completely negated their own advertising mantra and created feelings of animosity. So whenever you set policy on behalf of your company or not, think it through carefully and determine in advance what types of concessions you will be willing to make and which ones you won't make. Make sure your policies line up with your advertising or it could come back to haunt you later.

The Replacement Windows Example

After getting several estimates for replacement windows for one client, I chose a company whose program fit their budget and purchased 2 windows and 2 patio doors to be custom made, delivered and installed.

I was given a completion date, but it wasn't met. During the installation of the windows and doors, an inspector from the company showed up saying it was company policy to inspect everything.

But it was interesting that he never showed up again to inspect the work after it was completed. The client was dissatisfied with the job and I don't blame her. I was dissatisfied too.

171

After communicating dissatisfaction by phone and by fax, the company did not respond at all. Another phone call was made, but when the company finally responded two weeks had gone by.

The owners came out to the home and agreed that the work was sloppy and not done correctly. A new crew was sent to fix the problems. While the new crew was better than the original crew, even they fell short and a 3rd crew had to be summoned.

The owners of the company (while two very nice men) were not the people that did the work and you can see there was a lot to be desired in the final analysis. So when selecting sub contractors on behalf of your client or if giving recommendations, don't make your choices based on price or how much you like and trust the salesperson. Chances are you'll never see that salesman again so the proof of the pudding is in the quality of the crew.

Be sure to find out if the crew is made up of employees of the company or more sub contractors hired by the company. Find out how long they have been working for the company. If they have more than one crew, make arrangements to have the A-list crew from the get-go, even if you have to wait a little longer to get them.

Get plenty of references and do your research to find out who is good and who is not good.

The Carpenter Story

I have nothing against workers from other countries who don't speak English. Everyone has a right to earn a living. But you should know that if you cannot communicate with the crew, bad things can happen.

Recently I hired a painting company to replace the wood railing on an exterior 2nd floor balcony before painting the exterior of a home. It was a simple process of removing the present railing, building a new one having vertical wood supports all around the three sides, extending from the balcony floor up to the cross beam forming the railing top.

But what I didn't know is that the painting contractors hired another sub-contracting carpenter to do the balcony portion of the project who apparently never heard of the concept of a measuring tape and level and spoke no English.

When asked to approve the new railing, it was immediately apparent that the vertical slats were leaning to the left, so I pointed it out. The carpenter asked to return to the job site and adjust the slats.

Not once did the carpenter produce a level – I had to provide one and my associate had to teach him how to use it. His first mistake was in making the top railing too short. His second mistake was not making sure that the vertical slats were completely perpendicular and that once in perfect alignment, that they stayed that way.

After 3 return trips, the problem was finally corrected so the work could continue, but not without total dismay and frustration to all parties involved.

Find out in advance if the crew and you speak the same language. It is an enormous headache if you cannot communicate.

The Mold Repair Example

Out of a recent series of sub contractors that I have hired, I did find one jewel. On one project there was a pretty severe mold problem caused by a leaky toilet in an upstairs bathroom. The bathroom was located partially over the garage and partially over the staircase, beneath which was a wet bar adjacent to the garage.

To remove the mold, a specialized company had to be hired to tear out all of the damaged drywall, sanitize the area, dry the area and replace the walls with new drywall.

By chance I happened upon a gentleman who was top notch. He thoroughly understood the value of referrals and had great integrity. He also, fortunately, was bilingual so we could easily communicate and he quoted me a price for the project and I hired him.

He arrived on time – every time. He spent enormous hours on the project and I believe it took him longer than he had anticipated. But he never complained and he stood by his original quote to the penny. He went above and beyond the call of duty, staying late to get everything done. And he cleaned up thoroughly before he left the site.

I would have no hesitation whatsoever in recommending his services to other clients – none.

While I was very concerned about the quality of his work – and wanted a fair price too – I was equally concerned about his conduct and integrity throughout the process. In the end, it is his conduct and integrity that I will remember long term.

The Ritz-Carlton Service

Now contrast these examples. It's not that hard to run a company with precision and integrity. What is hard is to find other people who feel the same way you do.

The Ritz-Carlton is a luxury hotel chain that has pretty much mastered the art of excellent service. Their reputation is outstanding for that reason and upscale clients from all over the world choose to stay in their hotels as a result.

They have their own Credo. Copyright laws prevent me from giving you a copy here, but you can visit their site at http://www.ritzcarlton.com/

For our purposes here, I've taken some ideas they present and reworked them for the staging and redesign industry. You can refine it further to meet your own standards.

Our Sapphire Standards

Our Sapphire Standards are the foundation of our business. They encompass all of our values, including but not limited to our credo, our motto, our steps of service, our values and our promises to our clients.

Our Credo

_____ is a company where the foremost concern is the protection, privacy, timely and fruitful sale of our client's property. This is our highest mission.

We, therefore, pledge to provide the finest staging and redesign services for our clients to make sure every detail is addressed and resolved quickly and efficiently.

The _____ experience enlivens the home, instills a quiet well-being, emphasizes comfort and even solves the unexpressed wishes and desires of our clients without any fanfare.

Our Motto

At _____ "We are honest professionals serving ladies and gentlemen of exquisite taste and refinement." This motto exemplifies the anticipatory service provided by our company.

Our Steps of Service

- A warm and sincere greeting. Service begins with friendliness.
- Anticipation and fulfillment. We strive to resolve issues before our client's even know an issue existed.
- Long Term Caring. We consider ourselves more than advisors – we're also friends.

We Are Proud of Our Standards

- We build strong, lasting relationships and create _____ clients for life. We believe that's the only way to do business.
- We always try to anticipate expressed and non-expressed needs of our clients.
- We specialize in serving clients with discriminating tastes and who appreciate and deserve great service. We desire to make the process memorable and pleasurable.
- We hope to create a positive mystique that will last long after we are done, bringing true enrichment to the lives of our clients.
- We will always seek ways to improve our services, even creating innovative methods not available anywhere else.
- We resolve all problems quickly and without reservation.

- We not only work for you but with you, creating an atmosphere of teamwork so that all your needs are met.
- We strive to learn and grow continuously.
- We are involved in every detail from beginning to end, without exceptions
- We are proud of our professional appearance, behavior and communication style.
- We will at all times protect the privacy and rights of our clients as well as our company.
- We will at all time work in a clean and orderly manner, creating a safe and accident-free environment for ourselves, our clients and your potential buyers.

Our Promise to Our Clients

At _____, our clients are the most important individuals.

By applying the principles of trust, honesty, respect, integrity and commitment, we nurture and maximize the benefits to our clients and seek to retain their respect for a life time.

Chapter 11
Avoiding the Pseudo-Affluent

Who Are They?

Some people judge a book by its cover. I recently had someone complain because they didn't like the format of one of my books. Rather than investing time in the material presented within it, they decided if they didn't like the format, the contents wouldn't meet with their approval either.

How foolish when you stop to think about it, but somewhat understandable because that's how we're programmed to think. Some of the best training I have ever received in life came in less than professional formats. Yet I still encourage everyone to look professional, dress professional and act professional.

But don't think that just because someone dresses in expensive clothes that they are affluent. I think one of the things that has happened to us as a society is that we've all been conditioned by television and the movies to believe that all millionaires drive expensive cars and dress in furs and loads of diamonds and live in mansions.

Nothing could be further from the truth.

The truth is that most millionaires don't look like millionaires. They don't dress like you'd expect and they don't eat like you'd expect. As a matter of fact, they just look like average people.

Some wealthy people, as a matter of fact, <u>many</u> wealthy people would rather live obscure lives. They don't want to draw attention to the fact that they have money.

You can take any focus group on millionaires and chances are very good that the person conducting the focus group, or seminar or class, is dressed better than the wealthy people attending. According to one expert on the mindset of millionaires, Seiko (which is moderately priced for a watch) is the most popular brand of watch among CEOs of Fortune 500 companies. Another study found that the majority of men wearing expensive suits, costing hundreds of dollars, were men with incomes of around $25,000 per year.

Sales people often wear very expensive watches, far more than those they are trying to sell their services to.

So take note

People who are extremely well dressed are likely to be strapped for money, not the other way around.

People with extremely high incomes in America tend not to want to flaunt their wealth. So they live in moderate homes and drive moderate cars.

You can't even use the size of their homes as an indicator. The size and expense of the home is just an indication of the size and expense of owner's mortgage. They may be cash poor and over extended – and in America, most people are over-extended.

I can afford to live in a much larger and much more affluent neighborhood than I do. I can well afford a luxury car, or two or three. But I drive a PT Cruiser and I live in a modest, middleclass neighborhood. I have never felt the need to match someone else's expensive tastes and I can think of a whole lot better ways to spend my money than on a mortgage or car payment or any other types of products people might expect me to purchase.

When someone is conspicuous about displaying their wealth in the things they buy, it's really a better indication of what they owe, not what they have to spend.

Your efforts are to avoid those who are cash poor and over-burdened with credit debt and find the smaller segment who are wealthy but smart. They will have the money to hire you and won't blink an eye about it, so long as you give them great value and great service.

It's a fact: more people in the United States (and probably other countries as well) look wealthy – but they aren't truly wealthy because they have no discretionary dollars to spend.

Another interesting fact is that the prestige that is associated with a person's occupation often dictates what they spend money on and how much of their money they spend. I guess it's that competitive thing. I have to admit, as a professional stager and re-designer and a person who just loves to decorate, I do sometimes feel pressured to spend money on my décor related items because it would be expected of me. Still you have to do what's right for you regardless of what other people might expect.

Rest Easy

So now that you know the real target market doesn't dress expensively, tends not to drive fancy cars nor live in gargantuan homes, you can relax. You don't have to wear expensive clothes to impress them. And you don't have to show up for your appointment in a Lexus, BMW or high priced SUV to impress them.

As a matter of fact, showing up in moderately priced clothing that is well styled and driving a moderately priced vehicle is preferable. It doesn't send any signal to your prospect or client that you have made your wealth on the backs of people like them by overcharging for your services.

Rather, it sends a message that you are good at what you do, that you are professional, but that you are also fair minded when it comes to pricing your services.

And that's all anyone wants – great value at a fair price.

Chapter 12
How to Become Affluent

What Do You Want?

I'm going to assume that you would not have purchased this training manual were it not for the fact that you would like to add your name to the list of affluent, wealthy people in your community. You may already be at that level. But whether you are or you dream of that reality, you have the God-given ability to achieve your goals, whatever they might be.

Here briefly are some of the keys to get you where you want to go.

Acquire Knowledge

Many people who buy my basic staging or redesign tutorial never reach out for more training. My ego would like me to believe that it's because I wrote such strong compelling advice that they didn't need anything further.

But that's my ego.

The plain fact of the matter is that, as good as those tutorials are, they only give a portion of the type of overall training one should get to really become successful.

But since many, many people don't have what it takes to even do the basic stuff, there's no way they're going to come back for the in-depth stuff. And there you have it.

They don't realize that the truly successful entrepreneurs never stop getting training. The top professionals in any industry learn everything they can learn from their own industry; then they reach out to other industries and learn from them and translate what they learn over into their own industry.

However, remember, in this information-deluged generation, especially technologically, within one's own industry it's never really possible to learn all there is to learn, since the increase of available knowledge proceeds faster than our ability to absorb it. Fortunately you don't have to become a wizard in everything having to do with real estate. So relax. But you should know a little about the roles that various professionals play in buying and selling a home. Just know a little.

Then spend your best and most valuable research time getting to know staging and redesign inside and out.

I often have students buy the business training and think they are going to be successful on their design "instincts". Believe me. I've seen many a would-be self-taught stager/re-designer fall flat on her face in the design arena.

You see, you might look at an arrangement you've done and think it looks wonderful, because you did it and you did it according to what you know and how you feel.

But in actuality, what you've created might be ghastly in the eyes of true professionals who *really* know what they're doing.

If I had a dollar for every person who has called me in the last several years, claiming that they've been decorating for all their family and friends for years - why I'd be rich from that income alone.

The truth of the matter is that they may have made a suggestion once to a girlfriend about a pillow on the sofa, or they may have gone shopping with a cousin once, or they may have helped choose a paint color for the kitchen once. They also may have actually redecorated rooms or houses at various times, and received positive feedback. However, as in any industry, there's a vast difference between untrained amateurs and trained professionals. So the amateur "successes" can be personally fulfilling but not profession. Amateur successes can be fun – but they are only the successes of an amateur. Eventually it catches up to them.

That's not going to cut it!!!

I've had several people claim to have "natural talent". Then they apply for certification (without taking our design training), and either struggle with the exam and fail or turn in a portfolio that forces us to turn them down.

These people are living in a mythical world. They have not acquired the kind of training they should have and they are not only going out there and embarrassing themselves, they are making people angry.

Don't let that be your story.

If you don't have a degree in interior design already, and if you haven't taken our design training, get it done now. We have many inexpensive tutorials that will help you: *Décor Secrets Revealed, Where There's a Wall – There's a Way, Great Parties! Great Homes!, Arrange Your Stuff, The Secret Art of Hanging Art* – just to mention a few.

Beyond the basic business tutorials, we've got Advanced Redesign, a continuation primer for both businesses. You can subscribe to various industry magazines, visit websites (especially in real estate) and keep yourself "tuned up", so to speak.

You never know when a small tidbit that you picked up in an article or news clipping or another book will trigger the perfect statement to clinch a deal, or the perfect answer to a well-formed question by a prospect.

Pay attention to the little details. Donald Trump says, "God is in the details." I picked up that little phrase from one of the segments of "The Apprentice" and I've never forgotten it. It has caused me to gradually improve the quality of how I deliver my training materials and eventually will filter down to everything I produce and everything I do.

Rich people look for the small details because that's where quality separates itself from inferiority.

Acquire Technique

For every stager or re-designer, there is a technique to be developed. No two people will ever approach the business in the exact same way. Some people are real extroverts, love to party, are fearless when it comes to meeting new people.

Other people are introverts, shy personalities and cautious about meeting strangers. For them building a face-to-face relationship with a prospect will be more difficult.

But whether you are an extrovert or an introvert, one thing is clear. You've got to be proactive with your business or you will probably not last long in the business.

You cannot sit in a chat forum; you cannot sit at your computer; you cannot just build a website and expect the world to come to you. You've got to get up out of your chair, go out the door and make things happen. If you do that, you'll find a greater amount of respect for you as a professional and you'll also find that other people will respect you more as well.

Every time I'm in the market to buy a new car, I do what we all do – I visit showrooms and look at cars. I'm usually greeted by some over-anxious salesman who isn't much interested in what I want and need, just wants to close a deal. He's got his well-oiled sales pitch and delivers it with precision without ever finding out what I want or need.

If I don't find what I'm looking for, or if I'm not ready to make a decision yet, I usually ask and get the business card of the salesman. I must admit, however, I'm shocked at how few salesmen ever try to get my contact information in return.

In the 40 years I've been buying cars, I've only had one salesman follow up AFTER a sale. I've only had about 2 or 3 of them try to re-contact me after I left the lot.

The point is: car salesmen tend to be reactionary. Their natural tendency is to wait for people to arrive. If you don't buy from them at that moment, there is no follow-up and they don't seem to be interested in you anymore. They just want the business to fall into their laps.

This is not marketing. This is not proactive selling. This is "order taking". These types of salesmen are not likely to go anywhere with their careers. The super stagers and re-designers do not wait for business to phone them. They do not wait for prospects to answer to their postcard promotions. They are never idle. They go after the business – and you know what? They get it.

Look around your community. Find the affluent neighborhoods. Talk to the top sales people from the top real estate offices. Join the local organizations frequented by affluent people. As you start to incorporate these types of activities into your business life, you'll wake up one morning to discover that you have developed your own "technique".

Acquire Courage

Developing a successful business requires courage. There are no two ways about it. You have to have courage to start. You need courage to order your training and invest money in yourself. You need courage to speak out. It takes courage to ask for what you want. It takes courage to meet new people.

Most people have a great fear of rejection. It is this fear that stops them dead in their tracks. Because of it, they will manufacture all kinds of excuses for why they cannot go forward and why their business failed.

I was one of those people and at times, I still am. I am not comfortable in social settings where I do not already know people. I have to force myself to overcome my fears each and every time at the door.

Most people will find that the fear levels even increase more when they are face to face with wealthy people. Some of that is due to an over exaggeration of the importance of wealth and status, a kind of worthless "worship" of people who have money. And some of the fear is useful, because upscale prospects and clients are very sharp individuals. You have to be on your toes.

But to be successful as a stager or re-designer, you've got to be able to break the wall of rejection. You've got to respect your target market, but not worship them. They may be smart, experienced, and harder to please, but in the end they are just human beings with bank accounts. They have no greater worth as human beings than you or I.

The absolute best way to overcome your fears is to get out there and just do it. So what if you stumble all over your words. Next time you won't. So what if you made a mistake and didn't have the right answer. Next time you will. So what if the answer was, "No". Maybe next time the answer will also be, "No". So what? Maybe the next time it will be, "Yes".

Every "No" you get brings you just that much closer to your next "Yes". Be of good courage. Just do it.

To illustrate this, I'm reminded of my business partner who did a lot of high-rise, on-site cold calling when we first started one of our decorating businesses (Corporate Art Consulting). In the first two weeks, he made 500 calls, leaving business cards with receptionists, and received no appointments with the office managers. That's a lot of negative responses.

> Then, as he tells it,
>
> "As I was praying about this the Lord asked me if I was 'having any fun yet?' The obvious answer was "No!" His implied answer to my frustration was to <u>lighten up and enjoy the whole process of seeking new clients</u>.
>
> So He helped me make a slight adjustment in my attitude and I purposely <u>enjoyed </u>the next 500 calls over the second two weeks. They were also negative responses.
>
> At this point I had made 1000 cold calls with no positive responses. It would have been very easy to quit. But I was having too much fun!
>
> I had no competition.
>
> Then the following week I received my first "Yes". I went on to become the most successful corporate art consultant in the nation with the company I was associated with at the time."

Acquire Dedication

Dedication to your business venture is also a vital ingredient for success. All too often people start their training, then let the least bit of confusion, insecurity or degree of work involved blow them right out of the business before they even finish training.

Without dedication, you will let every breeze blow you hither and yon. You will give up when you need to press on. You will look back when you need to look forward. You will sit down when you need to stand up. You will retreat when you need to march. You will get hyperventilated when you need to breathe calmly.

No matter what life hands you, dedication to your dreams and goals will see you through the hard times.
There may be hard times.

There may be droughts.

Dedication will help you put your nose to the grind stone and plow ahead anyway. This is why setting reachable goals, both short term and long term, is so essential. If you have no goals, you have no glue holding you together, helping you be tenacious and dedicated.

So make a firm decision right now. Sit down and work out your business plan (see end of book for help with a business plan). Write it all out. Post it around your home or office. Look at it often. Adjust as necessary.

Stick around. You'll get there eventually.

Remember: Have fun and enjoy the process and the people in the process. This will keep your focus off of you and your fears and on to others, and you will be receptive to wisdom which your fear used to block.

Acquire Time

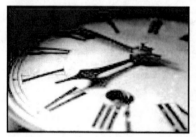

If you can, do this business full time. I'm not against part time entrepreneurs, but I think you'll make your business much harder if you do not commit full time hours to it.

It's hard to work on something, set it down and then pick it up again some time from now. It's just harder to focus, harder to build momentum, harder to stay excited and motivated.

You may have another job right now and you're doing this on the side. Or you may be a homemaker with children to tend to, and this will be a side business when they are in school.

Whatever the reasons you are not investing all your time and effort, they may be valid, but you need to know the road will be much more difficult as a result.

Time is money. That's why I hate it when I feel someone is wasting my time. I pride myself on putting procedures and policies in place that maximize my time. I don't have a choice. I've got to run an efficient ship. But it's also my nature to want to get a job done quickly so I can move on to the other tasks ahead of me.

When I'm writing a book, like today, I hate to be interrupted. A brief change of my focus inhibits my writing, my chain of thought. My staff has learned not to disturb me when I'm writing.

To be in business for yourself, you've got to protect your time.

There are two kinds of dishonest employees: money thieves and time thieves. Time thieves will arrive late and leave early. They will try to find ways to hide the fact that they are not working. They may even look for ways to falsify the time clock. Money thieves will steal money, supplies and other durable goods.

Prospects and clients can be money thieves and time thieves too. You have to know when to continue on and when you say, "No, I'm not going down that road."

If you don't value your time, no one else will value it and you will lose business right and left. So in every situation, you have to determine the worth of the client and just how far you're willing to accommodate them. Then stand your ground, even if you lose the sale.

Don't be so hungry that you're willing to let people walk all over you and run you ragged. Set your policies and stick by them.

Acquire Patience

This is a hard trait and I still struggle with it myself. I'm particularly prone to lose my patience when someone asks me for the same thing repeatedly and I've already responded repeatedly to their requests and yet I keep getting the same request over and over again. And having spent the better part of 6 years developing thorough information on the website for anyone to read, I get impatient with people who just refuse to read and then claim that I have deliberately misled them.

I'm only human. These types of things get to me though I try to rise above them. And it is something we all deal with, especially when waiting to reach our very first goals. You know the saying, I'm sure, "Rome wasn't build in a day."

Well, neither is a business.

I worked on my internet business for two years before I even launched it. Was I anxious? You bet. Was I impatient? Of course. But I've learned the value of patience (most of the time) and I know that some things just cannot be done over night.

Some people start staging businesses or redesign businesses with a huge bang. They know someone that gives them business. They get a referral right away. They have an immediate connection. Well, that's always great when it happens, but it can also be a hindrance.

You see, if you start off with a bang, you're likely to think it's always going to be going strong. Then when the market takes a down turn or you have a set back or some projects you thought you had got swiped away by a competitor, reality sets in.

The other day I was watching TV – one of the late night shows. Morgan Freeman, the actor, was the guest. The host had asked him about the history of his career. He talked for some time about the meteoric rise of some actors and contrasted that with his very slow rise to fame and fortune. He said quite frankly that he liked the fact that his career was slow and methodical.

Why, you ask - because he was well-grounded as a result. Slow and steady is almost always better than a fast rise followed by a quick demise, which happens more often than you would think.

When you start slowly, you have a chance to get better over time. You have a chance to set up your policies and procedures in a way that makes sense. You're never over-extended. You never develop a false sense of security. You learn the value of hard work expended over long hours and time. You have no delusions. You're reasoned, not rash.

Rapid progress also short circuits character development, whereas the gradual progress toward success is all about character development. You gain maturity and wisdom through life's ups and downs. Above all, the process hopefully helps us to live lives of gratitude.

Most businesses fail in the first 5 years, or so they say. In the staging and redesign business, that time frame is probably much shorter. It's not a reflection on the quality of training. It's almost always a reflection on the lack of staying power, false assumptions, laziness, fear and lack of planning and financial backing of the owner.

So if you really want to be successful, particularly with upscale clients, and build yourself a long-lasting career in this business, develop a thick shell of determination, cover it with fearless patience. Then go for it.

Keep a Sense of Humor

Lastly, be sure to keep your sense of humor. Don't take life so seriously. Be committed to building your business and reaching your dreams, but it's important to laugh along the way. It's healthy. You don't have very much in this life if you don't have good health, so protect yours.

Since I'm right at the forefront of the Baby Boomers (me on the left and my sister, Karen, on the right), I thought I'd stick in a few old jokes a friend just sent me. Hopefully they will put a smile on your face right now. It's up to you to keep the smile coming back later.

- Just before the funeral services, the undertaker came up to the very elderly widow and asked, "How old was your husband?" "98," she replied. "Two years older than me." "So you're 96," the undertaker commented. She responded, "Hardly worth going home, is it?"
- Reporters interviewing a 104-year-old woman: "And what do you think is the best thing about being 104?" the reporter asked. She simply replied, "No peer pressure."
- The nice thing about being senile is you can hide your own Easter eggs.
- I've sure gotten old! I've had two bypass surgeries, a hip replacement, new knees, fought prostate cancer and diabetes. I'm half blind, can't hear anything quieter than a jet engine, take 40 different medications that make me dizzy, winded, and subject to blackouts. Have bouts with dementia. Have poor circulation; hardly feel my hands and feet anymore. Can't remember if I'm 85 or 92. Have lost all my friends. But, thank God, I still have my driver's license.
- I feel like my body has gotten totally out of shape, so I got my doctor's permission to join a fitness club and start exercising. I decided to take an aerobics class for seniors. I bent, twisted, gyrated, jumped up and down, and perspired for an hour. But, by the time I got my leotards on, the class was over.
- An elderly woman decided to prepare her will and told her preacher she had two final requests. First, she wanted to be cremated, and second, she wanted her ashes scattered over Wal-Mart. "Wal-Mart " the preacher exclaimed. "Why Wal-Mart?"

She replied, "Then I'll be sure my daughters visit me twice a week."

- My memory's not as sharp as it used to be. Also, my memory's not as sharp as it used to be.
- Know how to prevent sagging? Just eat till the wrinkles fill out.
- These days about half the stuff in my shopping cart says, "For fast relief."
- Remember: You don't stop laughing because you grow old - you grow old because you stop laughing.

-- Author Unknown

Chapter 13
The Path to Affluent Living

Doing Your Business - Prospecting

OK, now that we've discussed all the ins and outs and theory, it's time to boil it all down for you into just the meat and potatoes of doing your business. So allow me to help you devise a quick system, if you will.

Scheduling Prospects

- Prospecting – Do it every day so there are no lag times and you don't ever feel desperate.
- On Sunday, decide how many face-to-face meetings you will have during the week. Schedule them all on Monday for the week.
- On Monday, schedule appointments for the entire week, and into the following week if necessary.
- Allow plenty of time for every appointment so you don't become frazzled and lose focus on the client you're with.
- Use a variety of methods for prospecting and to achieve the appointment goals: phone, post cards, letters, introductions out and about, social events, press releases, article writing, etc.

Creating Face to Face Opportunities

- Join networking groups
- Join industry groups where the affluent attend
- Join volunteer groups where the affluent volunteer
- Join clubs of the affluent
- Host parties
- Attend all parties to which you are invited when possible
- Introduce yourself when standing in line
- Introduce yourself when waiting in offices, elevators, restaurants and so forth

Creating a Pipeline of Referrals

- Contact centers of influence that you already know and get them to mentor you, giving you referrals at the same time
- Contact centers of influence that you don't know
- Speak to organizations about your services
- Join a networking group and give plenty of referrals – it will come back to you
- Contact local newspapers with articles of news and tips
- Write and send press releases to newspapers and magazines

Creating a Pipeline of Introductions

- Contact the heads of industry organizations locally
- Write letters to the editor of your major local publications
- Contact CPAs and Attorneys
- Contact the top salespeople in local real estate offices, luxury car dealerships, advertising agencies, property management firms

Filtering Your Prospects

- Qualify every lead and prospect (For specific training in this area, please get a copy of Home Staging for Profit or Rearrange It, my basic business tutorials.)
- Don't waste time on people with no discretionary income
- Don't overlook the soon-to-be affluent
- Long term relationships are more ideal than short term ones

Executing Your Prospecting Plan

- **Introductions** Strike up friendships with people in the industry groups you want to target. Get one or more to agree to mentor you and introduce you to key people within their industry group

- **Phone Calls with a Referral** If you can't get your mentor to give you a personal introduction, ask your mentor for a referral and ask why that person is being suggested. Does the prospect have a specific need you can fulfill? Does the referring party think the prospect will be interested in what you offer? Will the referring party call the prospect first and endorse you and tell the prospect to expect to hear from you? If you get a referral, don't try to have small talk with the prospect over the phone, like asking them "How are you doing today"? That's irritating.

Don't waste their time. Get straight to the point. Be sure to mention the person who referred you right away. State your reason for calling and ask to set up an appointment.

- **Phone Calls without a Referral** Try to first find some common ground upon which you can base a reason for calling them. If you have a specific reason, it turns it from a cold call to a "warm call". Identify yourself right away and state the reason for your call. I hate it when telemarketers pretend to be conducting a survey, or say they aren't trying to sell me something when I know they are. That's insulting. I also hate it when people call and ask for me, or my husband or the owner of the home and don't identify themselves first. Never give out personal information over the phone unless you already know the person you are speaking with.

- **Targeted, Exclusive Seminars** Don't let your seminars become a sales arena. Give quality information and tips and insider knowledge. This will show you are an expert and will cause them to seek you out rather than the other way around.

- **Getting in the Path of the Affluent** Proactively put your self in the path of affluent, wealthy prospects. You can't attract them if you never meet them. Don't expect them to come to you. You have to seek them, befriend them, get them to like you, get them to trust you, give them great advice and seek a long term relationship with them.

- **Self Introductions** Be prepared to introduce your self at a moment's notice. Have a one sentence description of your business ready to deliver. Have a 3 sentence description of your business ready to deliver. Never go anywhere without your business cards or promotional cards. Send out 10 promotional postcards per day. Do that every day. Collect other people's business cards. Send them a promotional card right away. Add them to your mailing list to receive tips on home decorating, real estate and staging.

- **Developing Small Talk** Create a list of questions you can ask strangers. Commit it to memory. If you are asking questions and showing genuine interest in another person, they are bound to like you and your fears will leave the moment you focus on the other person and not on yourself. Get comfortable with asking questions. People will tell you about their needs if you give them enough time to discuss their lives. One question brings an answer, which should lead to a follow up question, which brings another answer, which leads to another follow up question and so forth. When they are not around, write a quick summary of the information you gleaned. Contact them again if you've been given any time frame to do so.

Do's

- Study your own style of behavior – improve whatever needs improvement
- Smile a lot
- Be well rested
- Dress in a professional manner
- Ask questions
- Be interested in the answers
- Be genuine
- Have a great attitude
- Be flexible
- Avoid controversy
- Adapt your style to theirs – follow their lead
- Record all appointments immediately in a day timer or calendar
- Explain all promises and guarantees thoroughly
- Maintain contact through questions
- Notify client immediately if you cannot perform as promised
- Tell the truth. If you don't want to do divulge something, say "I can't discuss that."
- Always give good eye contact.
- Present a professional image at all times
- Take notes.
- Probe deeper into their needs with questions
- Use your experiences to illustrate points, even if they are not staging or redesign stories
- Use only factual stories. Never make anything up.
- If asked to do something outside your expertise, decline or say, "I don't handle that aspect of the business." Or "My schedule won't allow me to accommodate that."
- Establish your expectations early on
- Build a professional portfolio and carry with you at all times
- Always pre-plan you first few minutes
- Present your services in a seamless manner
- Clarify each "yes" answer by repeating what the client agrees to
- Expect to make several small closing statements or requests
- Handle objections by asking further questions
- Give specific dates of completion whenever possible but stating a range of dates is probably best
- Memorialize all agreements in writing. Give copy to client.
- Remember dates and signatures

- Keep on asking for introductions and referrals
- Plan each day's activities in advance
- Rate your progress at the end of each week, adjust accordingly
- Avoid Monday morning "blues" by checking off each task for the day as you accomplish it

Don'ts

- Don't assume anything
- Don't make their decisions for them
- Don't guess at anything
- Don't mumble their name because you forgot it
- Don't allow awkward silences
- Don't over dress or try too hard to be impressive
- Don't act like a fan just because they are affluent
- Don't stiffen up and become tongue tied - relax
- Don't intersperse conversation with "Ahhhhh"
- Don't cop a bad attitude
- Don't be afraid – enjoy yourself
- Don't bore them with your personal stories unless they relate as an explanation of some point
- Don't be manipulative
- Don't take notes on slips of paper – have a pad with you
- Don't say, "Trust me."
- Don't think to yourself, "How can I get out of here quickly?"
- Don't think, "They will never find out" if you're trying to conceal something
- Don't talk about controversial subjects
- Don't avoid eye contact, rustle papers, display nervous habits like finger tapping
- Don't chew gum
- Don't say you can't do something. Just say, "I'm overbooked" or "That is not one of my services. I'm sorry."
- Don't assume you have a friendship that doesn't need tending
- Don't get too personal with your questions
- Don't forget to ask for what you want
- Don't dominate any conversation
- Don't make up any stories
- Don't haul out brochures or other promotional pieces other than your business card
- Don't trump any story the prospect tells you
- Don't show frustration or impatience
- Don't scold prospects or clients for any reason

- Don't look disorganized
- Don't party the night before
- Don't assume a sale is confirmed – get it in writing
- Don't leave their home or office messy when you leave
- Don't forget to thank them for their time
- Don't assume that one mini close covers everything else
- Don't get thrown by objections
- Don't say you'll call them later to set an appointment – set it right then
- Don't neglect to write things down as you go or immediately afterwards
- Don't forget to send a thank you note or card
- Don't forget an appointment ever
- Don't be late to appointments
- Don't focus on what's in it for you

Accelerating Your Daily Activities

- Review all week's activities on Saturday
- Remove negative, time wasting activities for the future
- Evaluate positive activities and plan more of same
- Accelerate the positive activities so you have more of them each week
- Write notes – don't try to remember it all
- Adjust your business plan as necessary

Staying Focused

- Stay on task
- Disconnect from people in your life who are negative
- Stay clear of people who waste your time
- Have a goal for each week and don't reward yourself with time off unless you reach the goal
- Keep learning – ask questions, read, listen
- Check back regularly on our website for new aids, training specific or general help for your business

Planning Ahead

- Set short term goals
- Set long term goals
- Reward yourself every time you reach a goal

- Then reset your goals so you always have something to work toward
- Keep in regular contact with prospects and clients
- Be sure to thank everyone when you receive a referral or complete a project

Doing What You Plan

- Plan what you're going to do – in advance
- Do what you planned
- Evaluate what you did
- Adjust what you did
- Eliminate what didn't work
- Do more of what worked
- Do it every day
- Celebrate when you achieve short term goals
- Reset your short term goals
- Celebrate bigger when you reach long term goals
- Reset your long term goals
- Invest in your business
- Protect your health and family
- Become financially independent
- Save 10% of your profits for the future by investing
- Retire wealthy and happy

The Monday Morning Blues

There's an interesting emotion that usually hits most people, including me. It relates to a reluctance of getting started with your day on Monday morning. It's borne out of a fear generally – fear of failure and even fear of success. Monday morning blues could be a fear of prospecting, which is the fear of rejection. This type of Monday morning phenomena is not only predictable, but normal for many people.

Some people refer to it as the "Non Achievement Cycle". It's when you know you should begin prospecting for your appointments for the week but you start to think up all kinds of creative ideas as to why you should do something else instead.

If you don't break the cycle, you'll have to deal with it all the time. Sometimes you might win, but most times you'll probably give in to the fear and reluctance. If you give in, nothing will be achieved.

I don't have any magic wand to waive over you to make this go away but I suggest you do what my business partner did – make a decision to enjoy prospecting. Enjoy the people you will be meeting and speaking with throughout the day. You must be proactive in seeking prospects and turning them into clients, so you might as well enjoy the process. If you fail to prospect, you will be out of business instantly – which is the other way to solve your Monday morning blues. The only cure that I know of is to refuse to be distracted. You must be proactive in seeking prospects and turning them into clients. If you fail to do that, you will be out of business instantly.

As you read this book you are learning what to do. Now you have to follow through with what you know to do – and you have to do it every single day. You can't let outside distractions, your fears, criticism or anything else stop you.

The world is full of people who are unsuccessful. And the difference between those that are successful and those that are not is that <u>successful people are always willing to do the things that unsuccessful people are not willing to do</u>.

Successful people also are always willing to work longer hours. I said before that poor people want to be paid by the hour whereas rich people want to be paid for the accomplishment.

The old cliché is – No pain! No gain! – and your greatest pain may be getting over your fears and developing the habits of the rich. You've now learned how they think and how they act. So now you have the opportunity to be thinking, acting and succeeding just like they do.

To sum it up, you as a highly successful home stager or re-designer will do the following:

1. Get plenty of on-going face-to-face meetings with affluent prospects and clients week in and week out
2. Become a life-long friend and trusted adviser to clients
3. Stay in contact with your mentors, prospects and clients so you have the best chances of generating introductions and referrals from them.
4. Give more than promised.
5. Back your services and products with true, lasting value.

Treating Yourself

As you build your business, don't forget to treat yourself now and then. Treat your family members for their support and encouragement.

Periodically take some time off to rest and reflect on your business. It's amazing how quiet moments away from business can generate new ideas, tactics and procedures that will expand and grow your business even further.

All work and no play makes a stager or re-designer stale. Don't stifle your creativity by burn out. Make sure you plan time into your schedule for rest, for family, for spiritual input, for opportunities to give back, for fun.

Closing Comments

Your experience cannot and will not be the same as any other individual on the planet. To think so is foolish. A trainer could have thousands of successful students, and you could still fail. The reverse is also true.

The missing part of the equation is YOU. You are the X factor.

Do some of my students fail? Absolutely. But that is not my fault; it is their fault for lack of follow through, lack of tenacity, lack of determination and a whole host of other factors having nothing to do with me or what I taught them.

Do a lot of students, who take the high priced seminars, go away and fail. Absolutely. Many of them come to me groaning about how poor their seminar was and how they wasted their money. Many take my training secretly. Many leave my training and go take more training elsewhere too. I encourage that.

Do a lot of my students succeed? Absolutely. I've said it before and I'll say it again, "There is a dire need for staging and redesign services everywhere. The need is there – you just have to go find the right people and present them with the benefits at an affordable price." The measure of your success will be determined by you.

Does Harvard or Yale produce successful lawyers? Absolutely. Do they have students who flunk out or graduate and do nothing? Absolutely. Have their professors handled hundreds or thousands of cases and taught them the ups and downs? Absolutely. But they still produce people who fail - day in and day out just like the rest of the world. Because they cannot control what the students do with the information they teach any more than I can.

Some people chose their schools for the prestige. Does it mean they are excellent workers or entrepreneurs when done? Absolutely not.

My nephew decided to pay an very high price to attend Cambridge for his internship in international business. He believed he would be better able to land a high paying job because the name Cambridge would be added to his resume. The university's online brochure promised fame and glory. He's still looking for that job after 2 years.

Donald Trump picks each season some of the top applicants from all across the nation - literally out of millions of applications. Most are graduates of fine institutions, which have high percentages of well known graduates. Yet I'm totally amazed at how many of those who were selected to be on The Apprentice were unlikely candidates, who don't appear to have a clue as to what's important or what it takes to really become successful or who have atrocious people skills or a host of other weaknesses or poor attitudes. Some of them were highly successful on jobs or in developing their own companies, yet in that situation seemed to totally lack common sense.

None of that means anything because everyone's experience is different.

You're wise to look into the various programs available. But there comes a point when you have to say to yourself, "Look I'm going to make this work for me no matter what caliber of training I get and no matter who I select in the process. I think I'll start with this person, and then perhaps I'll do some follow up training with that person."

I've been self-employed for over 40 years and I still take additional training in a wide variety of subjects. Sometimes you learn a lot. Sometimes you learn a little, but that little can even take you much farther than you ever hoped or dreamed and the knowledge lasts a lifetime. On rare occasions someone will write me and say they learned nothing from one of my books or that it was priced too high. I've just given them the keys to wealth in a very creative field, and they think the price is too high.

Sometimes all you get is reminded of something you had learned previously but had forgotten to implement, so it winds up being a refresher course. Or sometimes you learn from one trainer what another had already taught you, but this time around a particular concept really penetrated and now you "got it". What's that worth? Plenty!

That's how education works.

You are the X factor. In the end, it's all up to you.

Training Courses

Diamond Deluxe Combo Program - Our most comprehensive training program, the Diamond Deluxe Combo gives you all of the training, tools of the trade, guaranteed certification and bonuses included in the Standard version; it also includes a custom stationery package. For details: http://www.decorate-redecorate.com/diamond-home-staging-combo.html

Diamond Standard Combo Program - Our 2nd most comprehensive training program, the Diamond Standard Combo Training Program gives you all of the training, tools of the trade, guaranteed certification and bonuses, and it also gives you the furniture sliders (8), the decorating organizer/tote and a package of full color redesign and staging postcards but they are not customizable. For details: http://www.decorate-redecorate.com/diamond-redesign-training.html

Gold Redesign and Gold Staging Programs - Get virtually all of our interior redesign or home staging training, our design training and the custom "tools of the trade" related to each business. Get VIP status with everything all at once. Two ebooks and the rest comes in hard copy formats. Includes guaranteed certification and a lifetime listing in our directory, plus a decorating organizer/tote. This program is for the truly serious and dedicated who want to earn career level income working full time but only want to focus on one business or the other, not both. For details on the **Gold Redesign Program**: http://www.decorate-redecorate.com/deluxe-redesign-training.html. For details on the **Gold Home Staging Program** visit: http://www.decorate-redecorate.com/gold-home-staging.html .

Silver Combo Program - Get all of our business and redesign training in one easy package. Includes all of our training ebooks and manuals for a packaged price but does not include any tools of the trade, promotional products, directory listings, certification. It's strictly training. For details: http://www.decorate-redecorate.com/silver-redesign-training.html

Individualized Training Options

- **Home Staging for Profit** - Our basic home staging ebook (or printed version) that covers all of the basics of how to start, grow and manage a home staging business. It covers marketing, organization, legalities, forms and such. Comes with 47 staging tricks report and some additional bonuses. Available through our Bronze Program. For details: http://www.decorate-redecorate.com/home-staging-training.
- **Getting Paid! Financial Strategies for Stagers** – This guide teaches you how to make sure you get paid for your expertise and labor on staging projects, which can extend over many days. When the economy is challenged, people are more tempted to avoid paying for services. Don't let that happen to you. For details: http://www.decorate-redecorate.com/getting-paid.html.
- **Rearrange It!** - Our basic redesign/staging ebook (or printed version) that covers all of the basics of how to start, grow and manage an interior redesign business. It covers marketing, organization, legalities, forms and such. Comes with free copy of "The Secret Art of Hanging Art" and the current "Color Trends Report". There is some additional training on home staging as well. Select ebook version or printed version. Available through our Bronze Program. For details: http://www.decorate-redecorate.com/rearrange.html **or** http://www.decorate-redecorate.com/redecorate.html
- **Advanced Redesign** – 187 pages of advanced redesign training to help you take your business to the next level. There are a wide variety of "tangents" that you can add to your overall business that all relate and complement one another. This ebook is available in printed format also. If you want to make exceptional income, this is a must read. Available thru Bronze Program. Select ebook version or printed version. http://www.decorate-redecorate.com/advanced-redesign.html
- **Décor Secrets Revealed** – 25 chapter Ebook on how to professionally arrange the furniture and accessories you already own or that a client owns. Step by step guidance covering interior design concepts for furniture and accessory arrangement (ebook only, not available in printed format). A must have for all re-designers unless you have a degree already in interior design. Having a "knack" is not enough. http://www.decorate-redecorate.com/decor.html

- **Arrange Your Stuff!** – 189 page manual (no ebook) of over 100 sketches (to scale) for actual furniture arrangements that will solve most room problems, together with page after page of actual rooms that have been redesigned. The problems of each room are pin-pointed, including my handwritten notes and textural descriptions. In many cases, there are several arrangements of the same room, together with before and after pictures. More details at: http://www.decorate-redecorate.com/arrange-your-stuff.html
- **101 Ways to Dress a Naked Wall** – Our exclusive soft cover book called "Where There's a Wall – There's a Way" (no ebook) is about to sell out but we are publishing an updated version called **Wall Groupings!**. 101 illustrations showing how to design wall groupings, both simple and elaborate, how to arrange around furniture and design gallery walls. Soft cover http://www.decorate-redecorate.com/book.html **or** http://www.decorate-redecorate.com/book2.html If this book is no longer available, there will be links there to the newer version.
- **Flower Power** – Whether you're decorating for a social event for your client or decorating your own home, knowing how to arrange flowers is a specialized talent you would do well to have. While we have some floral arranging training available in Advanced Redesign, you'll get the complete and thorough version in Flower Power. http://www.floraldesigntraining.com
- **Great Parties! Great Homes!** – Learn how to decorate for parties and social functions, how to be the perfect hostess and how to be the perfect guest. http://www.decorate-redecorate.com/planning-parties Great training for learning how to effectively promote your business and acquire referrals.

Tools of the Trade

- **Certified Redesign and Staging Specialist (CRS/CSS)** – Certification is not necessary for success, but some people really want that extra credibility so we have a private certification process for you. It involves an exam and submission of a portfolio to be judged by our panel of experts. Application fee. Apply here: http://www.decorate-redecorate.com/certified-redesigner.html
- **International Staging and Redesign Directory** – We get a huge amount of traffic daily to our website and many, many people view our online directory looking for someone to help

them with their home. For a nominal fee we will host your listing with contact information. Without the fee, you'll only receive a mention. It's good for business to be listed as someone trained through our program. Joining is as simple as filling out a form and paying the fee: ttp://www.homestaging4profit.com/join.html

- **Interior Redesign Powerpoint Presentation Slides and Script** – Don't try to "tell" people what you do – "show" them with our exclusive 60-slide Presentation. It comes with a full script which you can tailor to your situation. For use with Windows PC computers, whether or not you have PowerPoint. See http://www.decorate-redecorate.com/redesign-slides.html

- **Home Staging Powerpoint Presentation Slides and Script** – Another great tool, this multi-slide Presentation is great for use before real estate agents. It primarily promotes the services of a home stager, but ends with redesign as well. Comes with a script that you can edit for your own purposes. See http://www.decorate-redecorate.com/home-enhancement.html

- **Client Prospecting CDs** – Don't try to "tell" people what you do – "show" them with our Before and After Slideshow. It's loaded with a huge variety of pictures and benefits - the perfect way to turn a prospect into a client and makes it so much easier for you to sell the benefits of your services. Available in sets of 3, 6 or 12. See http://www.decorate-redecorate.com/get-clients.html

- **Furniture Arranging Kit** – One of the best overhead furniture arranging kits, you'll get around 1600 furniture decals to apply to special grid paper so you can create a bird's eye view of any room in your home or for a client. The furniture comes in multiple styles and sizes and all decals are reusable. See http://www.decorate-redecorate.com/furniture-arrangements.html For an Elevations Furniture Arranging Kit, visit http://www.decorate-redecorate.com/furniture-elevations.html

- **Furniture Sliders for Carpet or Hard Flooring** – Don't hurt your back moving heavy furniture. Do it the easy, effortless way with furniture sliders. We have them for both carpeted floors and hard floors. See http://www.decorate-redecorate.com/furniture-movers-carpet.html **or** http://www.decorate-redecorate.com/furniture-movers-hard-floors.html

- **Decorating Organizer/Tote** – It's hard enough to go shopping for your decorating projects and keep track of all your swatches and samples. We've got a very professional organizer/tote combination that makes it super easy. And you'll look classy too. See http://www.decorate-redecorate.com/decorating-shopper.html

- **Decorating Organizer Album** – Another organizer provides you with an album to keep all your receipts, photos, swatches, forms, measurements. See http://www.decorate-redecorate.com/decorating-organizer.html
- **Color Postcards** – Use our colorful, professionally printed color postcards to get the word out about your services. Cards are sold in sets and are generic. You must personalize them yourself on the back with your contact information with a stamp, label or handwritten note. See http://www.decorate-redecorate.com/postcards.html
- **Professional Work Aprons** – One size fits all black aprons that keep you looking professional and protect your clothing while working at a client's home. See http://www.decorate-redecorate.com/aprons.html for details and pictures.

Newsletters and Affiliate Partners

- **Decorating Newsletter** – While you're at it, sign up for our free Decorating Tips newsletter that comes out monthly. Send a blank email to join-ezine@decorating.listserve.us. You will be asked to confirm by our ListManager, so be sure to confirm and also be sure to white list our website and the server "decorating.listserve.us" at your email account to ensure you get the mail. Otherwise you might have to check your junk mail folder to find it.
- **Redesign/Staging Newsletter** – This newsletter is private and only available to those trainees that have purchased redesign/staging business training. We will enter your email address into this mailing list for you.

Other Training Available

- **Pro Art Consulting** – I worked the residential market as well as the corporate market. However, in the business world I offered my services as a corporate art consultant, specializing in designing decorative art programs for business facilities. If you want to work with business clients as well, this is a very low risk service to add. Select ebook version or printed version. http://www.decorate-redecorate.com/work-at-home.html

- **Floral Design Training** – One of the most exquisite accessories any home could have are beautiful floral arrangements, whether artificial or real. Even in your home staging business, don't forget about the importance of strategically placed floral arrangements. Want to learn how to create them professionally? Visit: http://www.floraldesigntraining.com

Contact Information

Barbara Jennings
Decorate-Redecorate.com
Box 2632, Costa Mesa, CA 92628-2632

Just as I have been teaching you to ask for referrals and testimonials, I myself would appreciate any testimonials and referrals you might share with me. Please write me and tell me what part of this manual has benefited you the most. If you are confused by any part, please let me know that too. And please tell your friends about Decorate-Redecorate.com. You will find contact information at this link: (http://www.decorate-redecorate.com/about.html).

If you find any errors in this manual or any links that do not work, I would appreciate it if you would take a minute and write me at the business contact address which you'll find at the link above.

Many thanks.

Bonus Section

113 Gold Nuggets Worth Remembering

I'm always reading and studying and researching and writing. And many times I run across tidbits that are simple but definitely worth noting and remembering. I thought you might like to read some of the concepts that have stuck with me through the years.

- If you make more money, you'll probably spend more money.
- If you target and understand how to service people who have money, you're likely to increase your own net worth.
- The affluent follow particular buying patterns.
- Stress is an important factor in the decision-making process of the luxury client.
- Sell wealthy client a concept and you'll be successful.
- Understanding how the affluent think will bring you higher fees as they will spend 82% more than other consumers.
- Successful people are professional and competent. They expect you to be no less than they are.
- Ten ways to guarantee failure are to offer: neglect, poor service, inefficiency, inconvenience, lack of knowledge, manipulation, deceit, failure to listen, technical terms, an impersonal relationship.
- Many people won't try to reach wealthy prospects because of fear and feelings of self-consciousness based on low self-esteem.
- The luxury prospect will generally listen to family and friends and look to them for referrals.
- Affluent people know you know they have money. That's why they are suspicious of anyone acting like a "salesman".
- Face-to-face communication is vital to success.
- The best way to gain status is through 3rd party endorsements.
- Referrals turn "cold calling" into "warm calling".
- True marketing is getting as close as possible to the target.
- You have to break up the horrible fear of rejection to find success in the marketplace.

- Avoid the pseudo-affluent but don't forget that many younger prospects will one day be affluent prospects. They are merely on their way up now. Build a long term relationship with them.
- Don't forget to contact rental agencies of apartments and condos. These people can give you great referrals and the average stager/designer never contacts them.
- Great gain can be had by those that study economic geography.
- Upscale prospects have respect for people with a high degree of knowledge. Learn everything you can about the industry.
- When specializing in an economic group, choose 2-3 industries whose downturns are independent of each other. One will, generally speaking, be up when others are down.
- Generating business for others will gain business for you.
- Other salespeople are some of the easiest people to sell to.
- If you give homeowners good reasons to sell, you'll have the project long before you competition even knows they are selling.
- Don't be reactive – become proactive.
- Being the first person to educate a client places you first in line to get their business and all their referrals.
- Research your target market to find out which sellers got offers below their asking price.
- When contacting a real estate brokerage, always pitch to the top seller first.
- It can take months and even years to win the confidence and respect of the affluent.
- Make friends – not clients.
- When buying luxury products yourself, insist on a reciprocal arrangement with your salesman.
- If you can get past the secretary, you'll probably be hired by the boss. Be tenacious.
- Use humor and good visuals.
- With rich people, don't try to sell on the first appointment.
- Target auctioneers right after an auction. That's when they are the most profitable targets.
- Spend your quality time marketing to people who have recently acquired a large sum of money, helping them understand the benefits they can gain if hiring you.
- Offer your redesign services to newlyweds.
- Obituaries are a great place to find heirs of wealth. Just before and just after inheriting wealth is when a buying frenzy occurs.
- Contact people mentioned in the press. They usually don't get anyone soliciting them for business.
- The truly rich have 10 million dollars of assets or more. Being a millionaire today is not what it used to be due to inflation.

- The quality of your character will ultimately determine your performance and your net worth.
- Finding the affluent is not enough – you have to attract them.
- Your income will only grow if you grow. How much you grow will also determine how much you gain.
- Your conditioned beliefs or childhood programming controls your thoughts.
- Your thoughts control how you feel.
- How you feel controls what you say.
- What you say controls what you do.
- What you do controls your results.
- If you want to change the results, change what you do.
- If you want to change what you do, change what you say.
- If you want to change what you say, change how you feel.
- If you want to change how you feel, change your conditioning.
- You can't change what you don't admit to.
- For every cause there is an effect. Change the cause and you change the effect.
- In a battle of emotions and logic, emotion will win.
- Homes are bought with emotions. Logic will be adjusted to fit the emotions.
- Affluent people believe they create life. Poor people think life happens to them and they are always victims of it.
- Money is valuable only when it has an effect. Where money has no effect, it is useless.
- Negativity and complaining will bring negative results into your life.
- Rich people do not consider themselves to be victims.
- Playing the game to win is different from playing the game to keep from losing.
- If you just want to be comfortable, you will never get wealthy.
- But if you are wealthy, you'll always be comfortable.
- Upscale people use their money to make money. Poor people use their money to exist.
- If you don't know where you're going in life, you'll wind up somewhere else.
- If you don't ask, you won't receive.
- You have to be committed to earning wealth in order to acquire it.
- If you do not value yourself, no one else will either.
- The marketplace will ultimately determine your value. You will be paid in direct proportion to that value.
- If you think small, your reward will be small.

- If you think big, your reward will be big, assuming you are not foolish.
- A poor person looks on problems as obstacles.
- A rich person looks on problems as opportunities to be overcome.
- If you resent rich people, you're likely to remain poor.
- If you admire rich people, you just might become rich too.
- Who you choose to associate with will determine what you become.
- Upscale people are not afraid to claim high value and promote themselves. Donald Trump wrote there is "no such thing as over-exposure."
- Losers are afraid to promote themselves.
- If you want to make money, be a leader, not a follower.
- Grow so that you are bigger than any problem facing you (and I don't mean physically).
- If your problems are bigger than you, it is because you are a small person.
- Learn to receive graciously. The affluent person knows how to receive.
- You will become what you say you are. If you feel you are unworthy, you will speak as one who is unworthy and so that is what you become.
- Having money will only surface who and what you truly are.
- How you handle little matters will dictate how you handle big matters. So if you have integrity in small matters, you will have integrity in large matters. If you don't, you won't.
- The wealthy seek to be paid based on the results they generate.
- Poor people want to be paid for their time.
- Working for someone else will usually rob you of the opportunity to earn what you're really worth.
- You determine your worth. If other people don't want to pay for it, let them fall away. Stick to what you are worth.
- Smart entrepreneurs offer both staging AND redesign because rich people think "both", not "either/or".
- Luxury prospects concentrate on their net worth, not on what's left over from a paycheck. Actually they often don't get a paycheck because they are entrepreneurs.
- Money is not the root of all evil. It is the love of money that corrupts minds and hearts, and generates evil in those minds and hearts.
- What you focus on is where you will strive. Where you strive is where your results will mass.
- The wealthy know how to manage money and do it well.

- Poor people know how to mismanage money and they also do it well.
- The wise possess their possessions; the foolish are possessed by their possessions.
- How you manage what you have is more important than how much you have. Save 10%. Invest 10%. Give away 10%. Live on what's left over.
- The luxury prospect looks for ways to make money work hard for them.
- The poor person looks for ways to work hard for little money.
- Fear does not stop the successful person. Losers never get past the fear.
- Dissatisfaction is the breeding ground of opportunity.
- Your selling skills must be so fine tuned, they are seamless.
- The best way to overcome face-to-face resistance is to "just do it".
- You don't have a 2nd chance to make that first impression.
- If they enjoy being with you, they will like you.
- If they like you, they will do business with you.
- Don't be too friendly, too knowledgeable or too anything.
- Trust in the foundation of everything you do.
- Professional respect is directly related to the manner in which you deliver services.
- Belief starts within you.
- Attitude is everything.
- Competition is good for the soul. Like it or not, it will make you better and keep you on your toes.
- Make a better product and you'll sell more.
- Give a better service and you'll sell more.
- Give better value and you'll last longer.

The All Important Business Plan

Since January 1st is right around the corner as I write this, I thought a discussion about Business Plans would be in order. Why is this important? Because if you don't know where you're going in life, you may get somewhere, but you won't know where you are. Writing your goals down and your plans for how to achieve your goals is an important step for any business person seriously wanting to move forward.

The stagers and re-designers and consultants who fail in the business are those who have never developed a clear plan for how they are going to succeed. I've included a ton of training in my tutorials on how to market your business and set it up and stuff. But yet people flounder because they can't overcome their fears and they don't take me seriously on the subject of business plans. The world is full of "wanna be's" who never make it, no matter how good the training is.

So if you haven't yet written your business plan and set your goals – set a goal to do so right now! The sooner the better. Until you do, you are not going anywhere soon. Your business plan will get you moving in the right direction on the right path and keep you focused and enthused.

Let's cover some basics

Your plan will define your business. Think of it like a resume on your business rather than about yourself. It should identify your goals. It will help you make business decisions, allocate your resources so you don't over spend. If you borrow money, it will govern how it is to be paid back. It will become part of your loan application. I once convinced a bank to give me a home loan based solely on my business plan. I also got approved for a $200,000 loan with no collateral from the Small Business Administration. A major part of my application was the submission of a 200 page Business Plan.

So if you doubt the benefits and power of a Business Plan, doubt no more. If the corporate world and the banking world hold them in such high esteem, why would you hesitate to get busy and put yours together?

Your business plan should provide specific and organized information about your company and informs others about your operation plans and goals. Quite simply: If you can't put together a business plan, you're in trouble as a business owner.

So don't drag your feet! Listen, I'm on my 10th book. As a matter of fact, I'm taking time away from writing it so that I can be helping you. Don't let me down. You don't have to be a whiz kid in English. I'm certainly not. And every time (just about) an English teacher buys one of my books, I'm apt to receive a complaint about my poor writing style, so we're all in the same boat there.

You're not out to win the Pulitzer Prize in Literature. You're just putting words to paper about you, your plans, your goals, your income, your anticipated expenses, how you're going to grow your business, how you're going to operate it and how you are going to succeed.

To get more specific, here are some core questions to ask yourself:

- What service or product does your business provide?
- What needs does your business fill?
- Who are your best potential customers?
- Why will your best potential customers buy from you?
- How will you reach these people so they know about your services?
- If you still need financial resources, where and how will you get them?

Once you have the answers to these questions, then create four sections:

1. Description of the business
2. Marketing
3. Finances
4. Management

Elements to be included:

- A cover sheet
- A statement of purpose
- A table of contents
- Description of business
- Marketing
- Competition
- Operating procedures
- Personnel
- Business insurance
- Financial data
- Loan applications
- Capital equipment and supply list
- Balance sheet
- Profit and loss statements
- Breakeven analysis
- Three year summary projection
- Analysis of cash flow
- Tax returns for past 3 years (personal, if not business)

- Personal financial statements
- Copies of legal documents: business license, resale license, lease
- Resumes of all principal owners/partners

I know, I know, I know. Looks exhaustive, huh?

You just take it step by step until it's done. Believe me, if I can write one, so can you. If you're not looking for financing, you can eliminate many of the elements above, but if you are looking for financing, a thorough business plan is the best step you can take to insure you get the loan.

Happily, in our industry, you really don't need much to start and grow your business unless you plan on buying inventory to stage empty homes. Most of you have a computer already that you can use when needed. If you can, take things in moderation and try to earn what you need rather than borrowing it.

Your business plan will show you (and others, if need be) whether your business stands an excellent chance to make profit or not. It will force you to take a realistic look at yourself and every phase of your business. It will help point out potential problems before they arise. It will help you solve those problems when they do arise as they will not be unexpected.

As your business grows and expands, you'll want to update your business plan, perhaps every 3-5 years. You can also use your business plan as a way to include family members so that everyone knows the goals and can work together to support you and those goals. And by writing everything down, you'll be amazed at how it helps you understand business, in general, and business in your chosen field in particular. You just may find out you've been going in the wrong direction or get confirmation that you're moving in the right direction. Whatever the result, it will be time and effort well spent, particularly at the end of one year and the beginning of the next.

Questions and Answers

QUESTION

Barbara- a few questions as I am going over your suggestions: - when you say "Cost of materials & outside labor are extra"- do you mean materials like paint, or do you mean materials like custom artwork, etc-

or are ALL accessories, including custom items like bedding, large items-mirrors/artwork, etc to be included in the initial pricing package I quote? Also- for live plants/potted flower bowls, etc- I get them at Home Depot, charge the client full price, then give them those receipts so they can exchange the plants if/when they need replacing- what do you think of this? - since area homes, esp over $1 mil. mark are taking longer than 90 days to sell, how would you suggest I handle "rental fees" for staging accessories I bring in after 90 days?- I feel there needs to be a time frame, my pricing would be for 90 days of use, then...???? - I am finding some sellers to be VERY controlling about their "stuff"- as in Feng Shui, I tell them that clutter stagnates energy, and we want to be clutter-free, but what do you do when sellers don't want you "touching" their stuff?...I specifically say in my agreement that "editing/de-cluttering" is sellers responsibility, because most people don't want someone else handling their family photos, etc- I guess it will be individual, but wanted to know if you find this to be an issue?? I guess I can include de-cluttering in my pricing, and deal with each situation as it arises? Again, thanks for your time on this!

ANSWER

Well, you see, I'm a big, big fan of making the whole process as easy as pie for them, with no hidden costs (or at least kept to a minimum). I really do think you're making it a whole lot more complicated than it need be and you could lose some people in the process.

Outside costs = paint, hardware, your labor force (painter, handyman, etc). You might even set a budget with them for these costs so they are aware of them with no surprises.

As for the rental of your things beyond 90 days, you need to pre-set an amount based on which program they choose. If you, for example, tack on $500 per day for services beyond 3 days, then you should have say a % add on rental per day/week/month, however you set it up. Try to pre-calculate how much you would typically put in a home 2000 sf or less and compare with how much they would pay for the furniture rental over 90 days and come up with a figure that is appropriate.

Don't give people so many choices.

The idea here is that you might make extra on some clients and lose some on others, but on the average you will make what you want. Before I had my present shopping cart, I had to pre-calculate in advance the shipping charges on my books and stuff. It is more expensive for me to UPS to the east coast than west coast. So I chose a base price to the mid-west or slightly beyond. My shipping was then an "average" price and everyone paid the same. Make sense? Now my cart goes straight to UPS and collects the actual charges, so everyone pays a different amount, but you can't always run your business that way, so you calculate an "average charge", knowing your profit will be +/- the average, but overall you'll come out ok.

If you're buying plants for them, give them the receipts and you're out of it. If they don't want to take possession of the plants, you will remove them at no charge, but there is no rebate on them. Again, eliminate choice. It's a big enough headache for them to think about moving and selling, so the fewer decisions they have to make the better (for most people). It also conveys silently to them that you're in charge. If they want you, they have to do things your way.

I've never ever had anyone refuse to let me touch their things . If you're getting that, then I think they are not viewing you as a professional consultant but more as a blue collar vendor. So you might want to rethink your image. How old are you? Maybe they think you are too young and something is making them nervous about you. In 40 years, I've never had anyone tell me not to touch their possessions.

So before that even becomes an issue, you need to address it on the front end and assure them that the greatest of care will be taken in rearranging their furniture and de-cluttering the space. Tell them you will treat their furnishings as you would your own and that everything will be packed carefully in storage boxes and labeled, etc.

Then you have to get tough and ask them what is more important to them: 1) whether the home looks like them with their personality (ego) 2) or whether they want to get the most money for their home (profit).

You have to assert yourself and let them know that de-cluttering will make the home look more spacious and not distract the buyers attention away from the home.

You've got to make it clear from the get-go that this is your goal and that everything you do will be to that end. Emphasize it again as you go thru your consult. Put it in writing too.

To your price sheet, you should prepare and attach a Policies Statement, which outlines what you expect from them, from the realtor, and from you. It should describe what is and isn't included in each of the programs. Out to the side you should have a short line regarding each major segment where you have them initial to prove this was discussed with them and they agreed to it.

The more you do on the front end to state YOUR WAY of doing business, the more you will find they will follow YOUR procedures and not try to control the situation.

Upscale clients will be more inclined to want to control you because they might look down on you and think of you as a lowly "vendor". They are accustomed to being in charge of other people and want to take charge of you.

That's why it's important that everything about you spells "I AM IN CHARGE. THIS IS MY BUSINESS. I KNOW WHAT I'M DOING!!!!"

By having all your ducks in a row regarding pricing, procedures, policies, expectations, and having it all in writing, you will go a long way to showing you are not low-end labor that can be bossed around, ordered around, disrespected and abused.

Believe me, they will respect you for your businesslike conduct and you'll get farther than if you come across as unsure, maneuverable, etc.

It's a process you may need to grow into, but you'll get there, I'm confident.

I think I wrote somewhere in my book or a blog that you don't want to convey "hunger" for the job. I have found that I have become more successful since I adopted the attitude that conveys this message: "I'm so busy and in such demand, I don't take just anyone. Here is how I work ...."

Then be absolutely willing to walk away from the project and be happy without it.

I have a much different philosophy from my husband and partner. Both of them are totally willing to do anything for any amount of money, no matter how little, believing that "something is better than nothing."

Not me!!!!

If someone doesn't want to pay MY price and follow MY lead, they can find someone else. End of story. I don't discount to anyone and I resent it if people ask for a discount. If someone tries to grind me, I walk away. I make far more money doing other tasks anyway, so I have never regretted walking away from a project which generated such obvious warning signals within me.

You may not be in that position - or rather, you may THINK you're not in that position. But you actually are. It's a mindset.

I refuse to do any project where I am paid below what I feel I am worth. Not everyone thinks I'm worth what I know I'm worth. That's fine. I don't need them. Their money isn't any greener than anyone else's.

So if you give in to the grinding - it will show up in your demeanor, your contracts, how you talk - all the subliminal avenues of communication - and you will not enjoy the project. Remember, the mindset of the grinder usually means that the grinding will extend to other areas and last throughout the duration of the project. Giving in to the initial pressure to discount shouts out that you have placed them in control and control will not likely be returned to you.

QUESTION
Hi Barbara- I am starting my brand new staging business and am having my first meeting with a client. I am a little worried about how to respond when they ask about my experience when I've had none! I am confident that I can do the job (and do it well) but how do I convey that? Also, do you ever find it easier to be the contact person with outside vendors or do you always leave that to the client? Thanks so much!

ANSWER
Kim, good for you!!! Questions about experience tend to only come up if you're portraying a lack of confidence in some manner or if you don't "look the part". I don't know how old you are, but if you're quite young, that can trigger questions, but in all the year's I've been in business, I can count on one hand the number of people who have asked me about my experience. That's because "experience" or the "aura of experience" exudes out of me! I look the part; I sound the part; I act the part. Now I can't guarantee you that they won't ask. No one can do that. But if you

handle yourself properly, chances are great that they won't. So what you want to do is not give it a chance to come up. You do that by launching immediately into finding out what they want. What's important to them? What are their goals? What do they feel are the most important problems they face? What is their timing? Get them talking. The more they talk, the more they like you. The more they talk, the more they feel important and that you care about them. Find out what they do for a living. Then ask them for a bunch of their business cards saying, "I'd love to pass you on to my other clients and friends". They will appreciate that gesture and think of you as someone that might make them money in more ways than one. I totally prefer letting the seller make contracts with other vendors on their own. It leaves me out of potential hassles. There are so many contractors and home repair people who screw up all the time, it's best if you stay out of it. Of course, if you do, you will lose out on some income. But I would develop a list of recommended companies and give the seller 2-5 options in each category. That way it's up to them to get bids and pick the one they feel will do the job the best. If you get reports that the vendor blew it, take them off the list.

QUESTION

I had a client, a few days later, have second thoughts about a ceiling color. They didn't think they would like the color and that it just wasn't going to work for them and wanted me to select another color. I did go back to select another color as a courtesy since I am trying to get some other business from her doing home staging because she's a realtor and I wanted to maintain a good rapport. She did offer to pay but I really wasn't there very long. I'm finding that people who have hired me once, continue to call for advice or want me to "stop by" for a quick question. I believe in giving them more than they expect which is what you've always taught but where do you draw the line. I also realize this business is strictly word of mouth so I try to do all I can for my clients, but I seem to be "giving away" more then I'm bringing in. I know it takes time and I have to find what works for me, but it does get frustrating. I so admire you in your business of so many facets. I can't imagine the time, energy and perseverance it took to get where you are today.

ANSWER

As for being taken advantage of, I have it happen to me from time to time.

I'll have people call up and try to quiz me on how to market their business without having purchased my training. So I talk in generalities and if they keep pressing me, I will eventually tell them, "Well, you're just going to have to buy my tutorial. All the answers are in there." That usually puts an end to it.

In your situation, it's kind of different with the real estate lady. If you feel this person can and will genuinely use you in the future or refer people to you, then you can cut her some slack, obviously. The last client I had who asked me to "come over, drop by" kind of thing was in an email, and I just ignored it. That's more difficult when they ask you over the phone or in person. I responded to her when she paid me for a 2nd full day - and I was there 11 hours but only charged her for 7. I clearly gave her more than I promised.

So your response could be something like, "Sure, I'll be happy to swing by the next time I'm in your area, but I don't know when that will be as I'm pretty swamped at the moment with half day appointments for my half day fee." This says you're totally willing, but that you won't make a special trip just for that and gently reminds them that you are in business for a fee, not for free.

You can also consider making up a brochure or flyer that you give everyone at the outset of your first appointment, which clearly spells out this type of situation and what you will or won't do. I've found in business that the more you can "head off" a situation, the better. Then it never even comes up.

If you don't want the expense of that, then when you first arrive, you clearly explain what you will do and at the end you tell them what "other people" have requested following an appointment and that while you'd love to be able to do that for them endlessly, you just won't have the time unless it is a fee-based appointment.

Or you could come up with a "follow-up appointment" rate, which you only allow each person to have once, and you assign a lesser fee for the "follow up". Doctors don't let you come back for the results of the test without charging you a 2nd fee unless it is already built into the price they originally charged you.

You could also have two types of consultations: one does not include any follow ups and a more expensive one does. In this arrangement, you might consider offering a two-follow-up plan or a three-follow-up plan with appropriate fees. In this way whether they choose the single, double or triple follow-up option, your time is paid for. A bonus is that many people forget what they purchased and never even call you. I'm reminded of the time I purchased fumigation services and was sold a return visit in 12 months for an additional fee. I chose not to take advantage of the option, so I wasted my money. But it was my choice.

But do remember that YOU are the one in charge. So you may be acting or speaking in some manner unconsciously that is inviting this tendency to take advantage of you. I think if you tighten up your policies and start communicating up front about some of these issues, you'll head them off in a professional manner and it will stop.

Potpourri of Simple Marketing Ideas

Before and After Party

Hold a "Before and After" Party in your home or a small meeting room. Invite prospects, friends, family and mentors. Use the musical slideshow CD with a large screen TV to present the services of redesign. Set up a small vignette with a chair, plants, fabrics, and a few accessories that coordinate and blend. Set up a room in your home with badly placed furniture and accessories. Redesign the whole room with the help of attendees so they can experience first hand the differences that great placement alone can make. Have your calendar handy to book appointments and offer them a small discount for booking at the party.

Home Staging Party

Contact a prospect with a home on the market who can't or won't pay you for your staging services. Ask to hold a home staging party at their home. Get them to invite a few good prospects to attend. Teach the concepts of staging and have them help you stage one room in the home. Have your calendar handy to book appointments or to at least collect their email addresses and phone numbers. Use these contacts to gain more introductions and referrals.

Color Clips for Keys as Promotional Tool

Pick up some colored key clips. They are attached to the various keys on a person's key ring to help them easily identify the different keys they carry in a purse or pocket. Use these clips as prospecting gifts or thank you gifts. Use them to introduce your services. You're guaranteed to be remembered favorably. Send a set of the color key clips with a press release to your local newspaper editors.

Live in Luxury While Staging

As a Home Manager you become a vital member of a growing team that is revolutionizing the way residential real estate is marketed. Your style,

 flair and fine furniture turns a vacant house into a valued home - a luxurious home that you enjoy at a cost far lower than you'd imagine.

Showhomes' mission is to help Home Owners and their Realtors® sell vacant houses. But selling an empty house is difficult. Buyers are often unable to visualize an empty space as a home. Your good taste and fine furniture enable potential buyers to visualize a furnished and decorated Showhome as their home, making it more likely that the home will sell.

As a Home Manager, you profit by enjoying an enviable, yet eminently affordable lifestyle. The Realtor always finds the home in show-to-sell condition. The Home Owner sells the home faster and for a higher price. All of the participants in the Showhomes program receive genuine value!

FINALLY A HOME THAT MATCHES YOUR FURNITURE

Once you decide to become a Home Manager, a Showhomes Placement Manager will work to find the house that reflects the style of your furniture. Their professional decorator will decorate the entire house at no cost to you. You keep the home in show-to-sell condition and allow Realtors to show the home to prospective buyers by appointment. Once the home sells, Showhomes will work to provide you with another luxurious home and to ensure a smooth move between Showhomes. In some cases, Home Managers are paid bonuses if the home sells quickly.

People become Home Managers for many reasons. Some need a short-term housing solution - for instance those who are building or shopping for a new home - and benefit from being a Home Manager for only a few months. Many become so captivated by the lifestyle, with its variety and affordable luxury, they continue year after year.

To qualify as a Home Manager you must:

- Complete a Home Manager application.
- Have fine furniture and accessories that will complement a Showhome.
- Pass their background checks (credit, criminal, and personal references).
- Be a non-smoker, and not own pets

Of course, you can also organize a similar program to this and be on the management end of your own recruitment service.

Manage Your Own Staging Complex

You know how some people open beauty parlors and rent stations to beauticians who bring their clientele into the shop to have their hair and nails done?

Well, you could do the same thing of sorts. If you live in a large metropolitan area where many stagers are performing services, consider opening a business suite. Rent space to individual stagers and re-designers who want to hang out in a professional setting rather than working from their homes. You can not only charge them rent, but charge them an additional fee each month for collective advertising of the services generated at that location. Your renters share the leads that are generated in a round robin manner and can even "partner" with each other as needed to manage projects. You collect your fees from what they pay you and it's your option whether you also collect a small percentage from all projects generated.

When trying to attract the wealthier clients, make sure that the facility is first class. You'll want to have plush offices, plus conference rooms and entry. Don't skimp. Create a restful, relaxing atmosphere and have plenty of quality brochures and visuals to show and distribute.

Visit Open Houses in Affluent Neighborhoods

By visiting the open house offerings of local real estate agents of wealthy clients, you can easily leave your business card for the agent. That's not the time or place to try to transact business for yourself, but it's a good way to start getting your services out to the right kinds of real estate agents. You'll quickly begin to develop a list of the agents who specialize serving the affluent and then you just concentrate on connecting with them for future partnering.

Figures and Distances to Know

Q. What size crown molding should I use in my room?
A. Figure a minimum of ½" per foot of height. i.e. 8' ceilings=4" crown molding minimum or 10' Room=minimum 5" crown and so on...

Q. How do I determine chandelier size in proportion to a table?
A. Dining Room-Diameter of chandelier should be a minimum of half the width of table plus 6"
i.e. 60" wide table=36" chandelier diameter

Q. How do I determine room size chandelier?
A. Room size is L (in feet) + W (in feet) converted to inches = minimum chandelier for 8 foot height room
For every foot over 8', add a minimum of 1"
i.e. 12 x 12 room w/ 8' ceiling=24" or 12 x 12 room with 12' ceiling=28"
A. Above a table; 28-36" from top of table to bottom of chandelier

Q. How high should I hang my chandelier?
A. For walking under; 78-80" from floor to bottom of chandelier

Q. What is optimum viewing for my analog TV?

- 27"- Six to seven feet
- 32"- Eight feet
- 36"- Nine feet
- 40"- Ten feet
- 45"- Eleven to twelve feet

Q. What is optimum viewing for Oversized TVs or HDTV?

- 30"- Six to seven feet
- 35"- Seven feet
- 45"- Nine feet
- 50"- Ten feet
- 55"- Eleven to twelve feet
- 60"- Twelve to thirteen feet

- 65"- Thirteen to fourteen feet

All distances listed are for eye protection but adjustments can be made by individual owners to suit lifestyle and preferences

A Few Upscale Product Sources

Here are some great resources to help you get designer discounts and or products that aren't the norm. Having access to exquisite products for this market will help you separate yourself from your competition.

The Guild
931 East Main Street
Madison, WI 53703-2955
Phone: 608-257-2590
Publishes catalog sourcebooks for architects and interior designers. Entries include lots of custom artisans of architectural glass, ceramics, mosaics, wall reliefs, architectural elements, atrium sculpture, public art, non-representational sculpture, representational sculpture, liturgical art, furniture, lighting, murals, trompe l'oeil, paintings and prints, fine art photography, metal wall art, mixed media wall art, fiber wall art. Artists can be commissioned.

Jessitt-Gold Interiors
1181 California Avenue Corona, CA 92881
Phone: 800-246-1990
A leading resource for window treatments. Provides catalog and free swatches.

Winn Devon Art Group – (800) 663-1166 – FAX (888) 744-8275, sales@encoreartgroup.com | 110-6311 Westminster Highway, Richmond, BC, Canada. This company is a trade only company and you can qualify for 50% off of their product by purchasing their catalog and setting up an account. To do that you only need provide them with a Resale License and a line of credit history. You can order their prints and have them custom framed for your clients. For the upscale client, you'll want to choose large mats and quality frames in keeping with the caliber of the home and taste of your client. Providing custom framed reproductions and posters is a great service to offer and you can even offer it to business clients as well. For training in how to start a corporate art consulting business, visit my website at the following link: http://www.decorate-redecorate.com/work-at-home.html

Bruce McGaw Graphics – (845) 353-8600 – FAX (845) 353-3155, sales@bmcgaw.com and for Canada sales@bmcgaw.ca | 389 W. Nyack Road, West Nyack, NY 10994. This is the company that published a number of my art images a few years ago, many of which are still being sold today in galleries around the country. You can purchase their catalog and get professional discounts of 50% off. Wholesale publishers like this always have minimum order amounts, and there are some penalties if you want to buy under the minimum, but you can still save a lot of money and purchase beautiful artwork for your clients and add even more profits to your business.

Petals – (800) 920-6000 | 730 E. Church Street, Martinsville, VA 24112 www.petals.com. This is a source for very nice floral arrangements. They publish a catalog which you can get for free. You can purchase ready-made floral arrangement and they have an affiliate program where you can purchase selected arrangements at a discount.

 **Autograph Foliages** – (800) 659-6151 | FAX (216) 881-3624 | 3631 Perkins Avenue, Cleveland, OH 44114 | sales@autographfoliages.com | www.autographfoliages.com. This manufacturer of beautiful artificial trees and plants also has showrooms at the Atlanta Merchandise Mart and the Dallas World Trade Center. They have a beautiful catalog of their merchandise for year round, plus they have a Christmas catalog where you can purchase ornaments and artificial Christmas trees to help you with your Christmas decorating services (assuming you plan to offer this service). If you purchase by the unit you get 25% off, by the tray you get 35% off, and by the case you get 40% off. The minimum order is $100 after your discount is taken. A $20 service charge will be applied to orders under the minimum.

Idaho Wood – (800) 635-1100 | FAX (208) 263-3102 | 3425 McGhee Road, Sandpoint, ID 83864 | idahowood@imbris.net | www.idahowood.com. Idaho Wood specializes in manufacturing beautiful lighting fixtures: landscape, street, post, wall, bollard, low & high voltage, interior/exterior and custom work too for designers and architects. Most products are, you guessed it, made with fine wood. Send for their free catalog.

Castec – (800) 828-2500 | FAX (800) 932-3323 | 7531 Coldwater Canyon Avenue, North Hollywood, CA 91604 | www.castec.com. Manufacturers of fine woven shades, you can order one of their promotional pieces, followed by a sample book for $150. They give a 100% money back guarantee which you can get if you're not happy with the sample book or their product line. And they are just one of many manufacturers of window treatments. Other companies to investigate are M & B, Hunter Douglas, Graber and Bali, and a whole lot more. A visit to your local hardware store, like Home Depot, will give you a wide assortment of window covering manufacturers and the contact information. Anyone proving they are in the design business can set up accounts and get usually 50% off the retail prices. This gives you a nice way to add extra profits to your bank account or order in props that you then rent out to your clientele.

Quick Fixes – When you need products (props) in a hurry and can't wait to order in what you need, you'll have to resort to retail stores, wholesale stores, discount stores, furniture rental agencies, designer showrooms and any other brick and mortar stores in your immediate vicinity.

Here are some of my personal favorites: Pier One, Cost Plus World Market, Macys, Mainly Seconds, The Alley, Pottery Barn, Z Galleries, Linens 'n Things, Bed/Bath and Beyond, Crate and Barrel, IKEA, upscale estate sales, upscale consignment stores, upscale auction houses, upscale antique stores, model home liquidated merchandise stores, better class department stores of all types, especially their "home stores".

Other sources (quality often questionable, and probably not that appropriate for the upscale home) are: Tuesday Morning, Kmart, Target, Marshalls, Ross, TJ Maxx, swap meets, 2nd hand stores, garage sales, ebay, consignment stores, government repossession outlets.

Remember, when serving the upscale market, your accessories must have quality (or at least perceived value at a higher level). When dealing with fabrics, look for fabrics with a sheen or high degree of rich texture: velvet, satin, silk, leather, suede. Your sofa and chair covers should be upper end deluxe models. Don't put junk into a luxury home.

Window Treatments – Window treatments should extend the full length of the windows and doors. None of this half baked layering up one side, across and down the other side where the fabric only extends down a short portion of the window or door (unless there is

 identical fabric beneath extending to the floor). That, in my opinion, is a horrible look and has no place whatsoever in a luxury home (or any home for that matter). I'm seeing more and more of it out in the marketplace and I think it's dreadful. I'd rather see bare windows than treatments that look like you ran out of fabric. Take your fabrics to the floor, please.

And while we're on the subject, please don't put strands of greenery up on the rods as a decorative element. Tacky.

To get up to speed, you'll find that many shutter manufacturers offer training to help you understand how shutters function and how to measure them, etc. Here are a few: Aveno Window Fashions, Comfortex Window Fashions, Dammer Custom Shutters, Hunter Douglas, Lafayette Venetian Blind Inc, Sunland Shutters, Sunburst Shutters, Vista Products.

The International Window Coverings Expo is the largest international industry event with over 275 exhibitors under one roof. To get on their mailing list, visit www.expoquestions.com.

CPSIA information can be obtained at www.ICGtesting.com
Printed in the USA
LVOW10s1514140615

442432LV00033B/1139/P